and we

worked

Happily

ever after

How Conscious-awareness can make our Work-life
a Journey of Happiness

Raj Bhambu
Anshu Choudhary

ISBN 9781095332375

We dedicate this book to our loving mother Mrs. Shakuntala Devi whose love, dedication, sincerity & hard-work as a mother and home-maker has always been our biggest source of inspiration & strength. She has always been an avid reader and we drew inspiration from her to develop our reading hobby and writing skills.

Contents

Preface

Happiness is both a feeling and state of mind which is within ourselves and is a choice because if we decide to be happy and are in conscious pursuit of happiness, we can certainly be eternally happy and it is a journey, not a destination. If we look to others for our happiness, we will never be happy. We ourselves and no other people or events or situations have the power to make us happy or unhappy. At the same time, if we are happy, then only we can make others happy, be it our family, social circle or colleagues and team-members at work.

What makes us happy at work? It is a question that each one of us and also many employers want to find right answer for. For majority of us, happiness at work-place is a mirage which, from time to time, we may feel is very near but seems rarely achievable. As per a prominent global survey, 55 to 80 percent of us see work-life as something to be endured and not enjoyed. This majority assumes that work is about stress and sustenance while we derive our true happiness from the rest of our life. For the rest, job is their entire life as if the rest of their life doesn't exist for them and they can't imagine themselves without work-life, oblivious of the fact that one day everything comes to an end, including work-life.

Many of us believe that success and growth are the key to happiness in work-life whereas it is generally the other way round i.e. happiness is the key to success and growth. In the journey of our work-life, happiness isn't a destination but it is journey and the direction which we take in that journey. True happiness can't be found in the abyss of unconscious ignorance and resultant automated, uncontrolled and illogical behaviours. It can only be achieved through being consciously aware of ourselves and our surroundings and using the same to engage in mindful behaviours.

Our happiness depends on how consciously aware we are and how we use our conscious awareness of work life, be it our priorities, needs, values, personality or those of other stakeholders or our conscious awareness of organizational culture and inner and outer synergies or dissonances. Gaining conscious awareness and utilizing the same in enabling us to engage in mindful behaviour or conduct and also conscientious and conscious decision-making, with respect to personal and work-life, results in inner peace and harmony and outer synergy leading to happiness as well as personal and professional growth.

Raj Bhambu

Anshu Choudhary

March 2019

Introduction

To enjoy the vast ocean and successfully traverse through the same, sailors need to learn not only sailing through tranquil sea but also surfing the high waves and tides. Similarly, to be happy at work-place, we need to improve our conscious awareness of every aspect of the work-life and be consciously aware at all times. Similar to the uncertainties of vast ocean, work-life has its own uncertainties, conflicts and dilemmas resulting in unhappiness and it has its own synergies resulting in happiness.

'and we worked Happily ever after' takes us through a series of steps towards being consciously aware in our work life leading to us being in a state of eternal happiness in the work-place. In our journey of happiness through improved conscious awareness, 'conscious self-awareness' i.e. our motivations, expectations, behaviours and moral or ethical values, is significantly more decisive and influential factor. Though, this remains a very important aspect in every human being's life, we will only focus on conscious self-awareness in the context of work life and how this facet of awareness leads to happiness for us.

Each one of us is different from others due to different personalities and consequent behaviours that we have. The conscious awareness about our work-personality along with those of others including colleagues, manager and other professionals at various hierarchical levels leads us to better understanding and acceptance of their behaviours and personalities.

Using the metaphor of 'concentric circles' we can be consciously aware as to how work location within corporate set-up impacts our work personalities and our preferences of work-place choices. Happiness is always related to locations, with familiar locations making us happier, but does it also hold true in case of work-place location and related work-environment?

Synergies always lead to peace of mind and resulting happiness whereas differences, dissonances and conflicts lead to inner and outer turmoil and consequent unhappiness among professionals and work-environment leading to reduced productivity at individual and team-level. We have dwelt on the possibilities of synergy or dissonance due to interplay of personalities to develop a better understanding of reasons behind dissonances and conflicts and how we can be more peaceful and happier through being consciously aware of reasons behind synergies or dissonances and how we can reduce those dissonances.

Sometimes we feel suffocated working in an existing team and the feeling might have started affecting not only our professional output but our mental peace and overall happiness too. We have focussed on this 'Black Swan' situation and how it affects our happiness or productivity and whether we can come out of it and if yes, how to do that.

Further, we shall look at the possibility, or not, of synergy between our personality and our manager's personality or our personality as managers which affects our expectations from team-members impacting us as well them. If there are possibilities of synergy, what can be done to improve that synergy? If there is no synergy, what can be done to reduce the dissonance? We keep wondering and grappling with a constant question or dilemma – Does my manager value me?

And this dilemma keeps affecting our happiness and peace of mind throughout work-life. We focus on this important dilemma to understand if our fears are just a misunderstanding or are actually true that we aren't valued by our manager. What should we do to make ourselves happy by either being valued or deciding to move out and when we should decide to move-out?

Work environment is affected by an organization's culture. Developing conscious awareness regarding our organization's culture and whether our personality and behaviour is or will be in sync with that culture type impacts our inner and outer synergies and resulting feelings of happiness. This understanding and conscious awareness about an organization's culture and our synergy with that culture enables us to guide our behaviours and actions to bring synergy and conscientious decision-making, if there are no possibilities of bringing synergies.

Having become consciously aware of all the facets of our work life separately, bringing all the facets together and becoming consciously aware of all these together helps us perceive work life with more knowledge, understanding and awareness and also helps us in understanding and being aware of our synergies or dissonances and reasons thereof. We can use this improved conscious awareness to engage in mindful behaviour or conduct and conscientious and conscious decision-making, with respect to personal and professional matters to bring inner peace, harmony and outer synergy leading to happiness and also personal and professional growth.

We end the book with discussing how we, as consciously aware professionals, can and should continually seek harmonious relationships with ourselves and also those around i.e. family, loved ones, friends, colleagues etc. because happiness is achieved when we are in harmony with ourselves as well as with the work-life and its various parts, be it people or work culture. We must do so through better knowledge, understanding and conscious awareness of our inner and outer self and surrounding environment, be it family, social or work-life.

1. Happiness and Conscious Awareness

"Happiness is the meaning and purpose of life, the whole aim and end of human existence." - Aristotle

Have we ever reflected as to what is happiness for us; is it a feeling or a state of mind; is it within ourselves or something outside of ourselves; is happiness a choice or not; is it a destination or a journey; is it a commodity; is it an event; does it occur by accident; is it transitory or can it be eternal; what makes us happy; can we control our happiness or it has to be dependent on outside factors always? We all have different answers to each of these questions because we rarely delve deeper into understanding what happiness means for us.

Happiness is a feeling, state of mind and something within us, is a choice and a journey. Happiness is neither a commodity nor an event not it occurs by accident. It is an ongoing process and is basically our mind-set, attitude and psyche. If we live a life where we have inner peace of mind, harmony within and harmony with our surrounding environment, then happiness flows from there. We can live in an eternal feeling of happiness and for that we should always determine it ourselves as to what happiness means for us.

There are several factors which contribute to happiness for us and those factors keep varying depending on each of us as individuals, time, place and situation. More often than not, it is our tendency to designate external things as happiness destination, which makes happiness such a transitory feeling for us. When we achieve, what we felt would make us happy, we shift our happiness destination to something else. Till the time, we keep earmarking happiness destinations or something that is outside us, we will always be unhappy because ultimately happiness is a journey, not destinations. It is our feeling and state of mind so must be something internal to us. Therefore, it is important for us to know, understand, internalize and become conscious of as to what makes us happy without connecting it to external things.

Peace of mind leads to happiness and whatever disturbs our peace of mind works as a factor in our unhappy feeling or state of mind. Without peace of mind, nothing else has much value and each of us strive to achieve peace of mind throughout our life. Ignorance and inner conflicts, mismatch between our inner motivations or related expectations and what we achieve, incoherent moral and ethical values, dissonance between what we want to say or do and what we actually say or do, conflicts or differences with people around us or the environment we exist in, contribute to restlessness and disturb our peace of mind and happiness. Removal or reduction of inner and outer dissonances and conflicts lead us towards right direction in our journey happiness because we tend to achieve our peace of mind in absence of dissonances and conflicts.

Whenever we interact with other human beings in our personal, social or work-life, those interactions result in either synergies or differences. Everyone feels happy when there are synergies in these interactions whereas differences, after a threshold which varies from individual to individual, lead to conflicts and those conflicts always result in a feeling of unhappiness for us as well as others.

Apart from people around us, our perceived synergies or dissonances with our physical, social and cultural environment impacts our happiness. We feel happy when we perceive that our ethical or moral values and other related aspects of the environment are as per our expectations and we tend to lose our peace of mind when there are significant dissonances with the environment.

In the context of our work-life, our happiness depends on our perception of the work-life which, in turn, depends on three aspects i.e. knowledge, awareness and consciousness. In the absence of either or all of these three aspects, we are prone to develop prejudiced perceptions and consequent irrational behaviours and decisions which affect our happiness at the work-place and the same, more often than not, spills to our personal life.

'Knowledge' implies how much understanding, comprehension, grasp or intelligence we have about corporate work-settings. 'Awareness' is the result or response of the exchange of information between our sensing apparatus (five senses) and the knowledge or intelligence we have. 'Consciousness' is the state of being aware and being positively responsive to what is happening around us.

To explain the differentiation further, we might be knowing and aware of some unethical practices in our organization but are we conscious of those practices i.e. are we only aware or are we in a state of being conscious about the adverse effects these unethical practices might have on our life and career and what we should be doing about the same?

The fourth dimension is 'Conscious Awareness' which is the mental state of being truly aware of events and situations in our work life and effect these events or situations have on us and also on others. Conscious awareness is not only about being consciously aware of outside behaviours, environment or culture but also being consciously aware of our personality, feelings, expectations, motivations, behaviours and actions or reactions i.e. 'conscious self-awareness'.

For us, the key to achieving true internal happiness, satisfaction and fulfilment our expectations from a job depends on three factors:

Firstly, how consciously self-aware we are about what matters to us in terms of inner motivational needs, values, standards, priorities etc. and whether or not, we have 'organized our behaviours and habits' in accordance to what matters to us internally;

Secondly, how consciously aware we are about our personality, other's personalities, interplay of personalities resulting in either synergy or dissonance, our and other work-place environments or cultures, synergy or dissonance between our values, standards, behaviours, expectations and work culture of our organization; and

Thirdly, how we use this 'conscious awareness' to guide our behavioural actions or reactions and professional or personal decision-making in the work-setting to bring inner and outer synergy because we can achieve happiness only through acceptance and inner and outer synergy. Our choices and decisions have a big impact on our happiness. Conscious awareness enables us to make informed choices and conscientious decisions to bring harmony and happiness in our lives.

We must be objective in our journey of conscious awareness because used negatively, it can convert us to being essentially self-absorbed. In that case, we might use it internally and externally to justify our every thought and action and filter them through our individual biases. This will lead us in the opposite direction on the happiness journey and we will be farther and farther away from the desired state of happiness.

Our past and future aren't always better than our present. Yet we continue to think that is the case. Conscious awareness makes us work and live happily in the present situation with maximum possible synergies.

> *"The key to growth is the production of higher dimensions of consciousness into our awareness." - Lao Tzu*

2. Knowing Ourselves

"He who lives in harmony with himself, lives in harmony with the universe." – Marcus Aurelius

The most difficult thing in life is to know ourselves. To feel happy and perform to best of our abilities, we need to know who we are, what we think, why we think, feel and act or react the way we do. Self-awareness goes hand in hand with inner happiness, positive thinking and outer achievement.

Apart from the ever-existing focus of philosophical and religious texts on this important aspect, the psychological study of self-awareness can be traced back to 1972 when psychologists Shelley Duval and Robert Wicklund developed the theory of self-awareness. They proposed that "when we focus our attention on ourselves, we evaluate and compare our current behaviour to our internal standards and values. We become self-conscious as objective evaluators of ourselves". In essence they considered self-awareness as a major mechanism of self-control. Psychologist Daniel Goleman had proposed a more popular definition of self-awareness as knowing our internal states, preferences, resources and intuitions.

Apart from these, a lot has been said and written about self-awareness by psychologists, philosophers and spiritual speakers or authors. If we know everything external and nothing internal, then we are the most ignorant one. Similarly, if we know everything external as well as internal, but are neither consciously aware about that knowledge nor understands how to use that knowledge to bring peace and harmony in our lives and other's lives, we are no better than an ignorant person. Then, our situation is similar to us standing in the rains with an umbrella in our hand but neither knowing what is the use of that umbrella nor protecting ourselves from the rains.

In the journey of improving our conscious awareness, 'conscious self-awareness' is significantly more decisive and influential factor. Conscious self-awareness is much more than self-awareness which is knowing our internal states, intuitions, behaviours, preferences, resources, internal standards and values. It is about objective understanding of our behaviours, values, beliefs or opinions and not understanding ourselves based on other people's opinions and views. Other people may affect our objectivity either through excess praise or through constant criticism.

Though, this remains a very important aspect in every human being's life, we will only focus on conscious self-awareness in the context of work life. Conscious self-awareness encompasses being consciously aware of our external behaviours or personality and also internal standards and values i.e. 'what matters to us' internally and knowing how we can use this knowledge to effect changes. Our harmony or synergy depends a lot on - whether or not, we have 'organized our behaviours and habits' in accordance to what matters to us internally i.e. our internal standards, values, priorities etc., knowing all these and being consciously aware of these. This empowers us to understand ourselves better, being at peace with who we are and proactively managing or changing our thoughts and behaviours to bring more inner harmony and synergy with our surrounding environment. This is so because we can make significant changes or adaptations in our thought processes or behaviours only after being consciously self-aware.

What Matters the Most in Our Life?

The first logical step in the conscious awareness journey would be to understand and become consciously aware of - 'what matters most in our life' and have we organized our life i.e. activities, behaviours, actions and reactions, accordingly? When we understand what matters to us, it will help consolidate and substantiate our conscious self-awareness. This knowledge will further accentuate overall conscious self-awareness once we realize and understand whether our existing inner and outer dissonance is a result of conflict between inner priorities, preferences, standards or values and outer or actual behaviours, priorities, values etc.

At different points of our life, different things take importance. So, in school or college, it was grades and friends that mattered the most, after college, it was getting a job and thus our priorities keep changing. However, at the most basic level, our priorities are dependent on the personality that we have developed. If we attach our happiness to these priorities as being happiness destinations, then similar to these priorities, happiness will obviously be transitory and not eternal.

To understand and know as to what matters most in our life, we can start from the very basics. Every individual's life has some basic facets i.e. 'personal' comprising of family, 'social' comprising of relatives, friends, neighbours, and acquaintances etc., 'economic' comprising of one or multiple means of earning livelihood i.e. job, business or both, 'political' comprising of either only political views or active political participation. Have we ever wondered what matters most to us among these various facets of life?

A simple paper and pencil exercise at this juncture will be helpful. Let us prioritize the various facets of our life by putting the top-most priority item as number one and the one with least priority as last item on the list. Let us leave this list to rest for some time and forget about this list. Now, let us focus on the actual behaviours, time spent and focus, attention and importance provided to each activity through our behaviours. Our every behaviour or focus-span is indicative of some or other facet of our life. For example, if we are working eight hours a day, commuting two hours and then bringing home office work of another two hours, then we are spending twelve hours a day on economic activity i.e. earning a livelihood. Based on such a conscious analysis of our behaviour, let us list-out the various facets of life with those getting maximum actual effort, time, focus, attention and importance being listed as top priority and the one with least effort, time, focus and attention being listed as the last item.

Comparing the two lists i.e. what we think should matter to us in our life or be our priorities and what does our behaviour point to as being our actual priorities, we may find either synergies and harmony or a lot of dissonance. This dissonance, between our inner priorities and actual priorities being reflected in our behaviours, is the first reason of our unhappiness.

> *A conscious awareness of our priorities in life and organizing our behaviours accordingly helps us in bringing lot of inner and outer synergies in our personal, professional and social life. And we must always remember that irrespective of people, personalities, or situations, synergies lead to happiness while dissonance always results in unhappiness.*

The analysis of our priorities in life and consequent synergies or dissonances is at the macro-level and we can always go deeper analysing various parts of each of the facets i.e. personals, social, economic or political to understand and improve our self-awareness. For example, our 'personal' facet consists of ourselves, parents, siblings, wife and children. Within this personal space, a conscious awareness of whether we are able to maintain harmony between priorities at inner and behaviour level and resulting synergy or dissonance helps us in effecting changes to bring more harmony and inner peace.

If we keenly watch behaviours of ourselves and our colleagues, it seems as if for some, a job is an economic activity i.e. means to earn a living; for others, it seems to be their entire life wherein they seem to have forgotten everything but their job; for a few others, it seems like an ego-satisfying social exercise through higher designations or material acquisitions; while for some others, it seem to be part of a never-ending race of occupying higher positions and trying to reach the top position whichever they can visualize. Behaviours and activities of each of us point to how we have organized our work lives. For us, it is important to understand why we took-up a job and became professionals in the first place.

As professionals, are we consciously aware of the basic question i.e. 'what we want from our job' and answer thereof. We can better look at this question from another angle i.e. what is our motivation to take-up and continue in a job? Highlighting our motivations through outwardly visible behaviours in work-life but to not being consciously self-aware of the same is foolish and unreasonable. Without knowing ourselves and being consciously aware, we will get nowhere. To show us a way, even Google maps first ask us our location. In life, despite our professional success, we often suffer private failures because throughout, we had set wrong priority of needs which was in contradiction to priority of needs synergized with our inner self.

Priority of Needs in Work-Life

One of the best known and the most widely studied work-place motivational theories is Maslow's Hierarchy of Needs, a theory proposed by Abraham Maslow in his 1943 paper titled "A Theory of Human Motivation" and his subsequent book 'Motivation and Personality'. The hierarchy of needs proposed by Maslow from lower to higher levels was – Physiological (food, shelter), Safety (safe working environment, job security), Social (feeling wanted, sense of belonging, part of team), Esteem (recognition, status, importance, respect) and Self-Actualization (value based, intellectual needs, fulfilling potential, achieving targets).

This hierarchy suggests that people are motivated to fulfil basic needs before moving on to other, more advanced needs. Though the hierarchy is portrayed as fairly rigid, Maslow noted that the order in which these needs are fulfilled doesn't always follow this progression from lower to higher. For example, for some individuals the need for self-esteem is much more than the need for love. In work places, human resources people and leaders at various levels use this theory to keep their teams motivated. This way an outer entity i.e. organization (HR people or leader) is trying to ascertain our needs and what motivates us, so that they can utilize our potential and that's good as far as it is being done positively with positive results for both sides.

Our motivational needs can be delved into from different perspectives but we are using this model as a reference point because it happens to be most widely used and studied. Ultimately, the aim is to bring conscious awareness about 'what matters to us as professionals' and have we prioritized 'what matters to us' based on our conscious self-awareness. Also, have we organized our behaviour accordingly or there is a complete dissonance within priorities and resultant behaviours leading to inner and outer conflicts.

> *Conscious self-awareness is the state in which we know, understand and become consciously self-aware as to what are our motivational needs and priorities for doing the job? This is where our conscious awareness of 'what matters to us' becomes important.*

A lot of times, not being consciously aware of what matters to us leads to wrong priorities and consequent dissonances and unhappiness. Let us look at each motivational need from our perspective in the work-life context.

Physiological needs

Physiological needs are biological requirements for human survival i.e. food, shelter, clothing etc. For us, more often than not, food, shelter and clothing, as a basic need, is generally fulfilled. But mostly, the definition of basic needs keeps shifting as we make materialistic progress in life. So, it may be different for different people. In this context, let us assume what we can afford today as far as our basic needs i.e. food, shelter and clothing are concerned are our physiological needs.

Is fulfilment of our physiological needs of food, shelter and clothing, the reason we are doing a job? To understand it better, let us ask ourselves – will these basic needs be adversely affected if we don't have the job we are doing? If we have other means of livelihood or investments which are sufficient to take care of these basic needs and those other means aren't dependent on the continuity of this job, then certainly physiological need may not be the motivational need for the job. If there are no other means, then a job is very much the basic requirement to fulfil our physiological needs. Even Maslow considered physiological needs as the most important since all other needs become secondary until these needs are met.

If fulfilment of our physiological needs depends on the job, we must to be consciously self-aware that 'having a job does matter' and is a priority. So, job security is of utmost importance to us in such a scenario. However, this conscious self-awareness shouldn't propel us towards always being fearful of losing our job and resultant unethical behavioural changes. This conscious awareness is more helpful in knowing that a job is a basic requirement, though it doesn't have to be this very job that we are doing. Whether it has to be in this job or some other job, is a separate decision altogether and should be taken after due considerations, based on our conscious awareness of multiple factors that we will be discussing later.

Looking at the negative effect of the conscious awareness that job is a physiological need, as mentioned above, it might make us fearful of losing our job. This fear further makes us too meek, agreeable and constantly trying to save our job. Most of the times, this factor and the resultant behaviour of ours makes the work place a highly stressful, too agreeable and unethical place with no human values. We must keep these negative thoughts out of our mind because, as said earlier, a job may a physiological need but it doesn't have to be this very job.

Safety Needs

In the work-life context, safety needs refer to physical safety i.e. safety from dangers to life, economic safety i.e. safety from fear of losing our job and legal safety i.e. safety from any legal action on account of doing something as part of corporate job which means doing only legally compliant work.

Does our motivation in a job a result of fulfilment of these safety needs? Being consciously self-aware of objective and truthful answers to some questions might help us find-out whether safety needs matter to us and are a priority thereof. Are we willing to take-up a job-role that doesn't emphasize physical safety of its employees or a company or organization which doesn't have good record of employee safety? Are we motivated to take-up a job with a company having very high attrition rate or frequent forced exits or resignations? Are we ready to work for a company which is infamous for its legal non-compliances or one that is profit-oriented at the cost of legal compliances?

If the answer to above questions is 'NO', then our motivation and what matters to us is fulfilment of 'safety needs'. A conscious self-awareness regarding importance of this need will help us in prioritizing our actions, behaviours and activities and making crucial decisions.

Social Needs

In the work-life context, social needs refer to need for interpersonal relationships and a sense of belongingness. This might be motivational need of looking for interpersonal relationships such as friendships etc. in our organization or a sense of belonging to our team or sense of belonging to our organization. We often hears the words my friend, my team, my company etc. in work life and this feeling affecting motivation of a lot of us to indulge in certain action, behaviours or activities.

Let us look for answers to a few questions to ascertain whether we are trying to fulfil our social needs and giving importance to our resultant behaviours in work life.

Are our decisions being affected by, or we think we are making sacrifices for, certain colleagues and team-members whom we assume to be our friends? Does our social life outside our work life gets less priority compared to our work place social life? Are we trying to compensate for lack of personal social life through over-involvement in work place social life?

If the answer to above questions is 'Yes', then we need to be consciously aware that we are trying to meet our social needs in the job itself. In that case, the job might have assumed far more importance in our life without us being consciously aware of the situation as to what will happen when there is no job or change of work-place, job and organization.

> *A conscious self-awareness of the importance of fulfilling our social needs in work life and prioritizing the same might help us avoid over-emphasizing this aspect in work life and adverse impact it might have on our professional as well as personal and social life. This doesn't mean that we shouldn't have a sense of belongingness to our team or organization but this conscious awareness helps us avoid the extremes.*

Every organization expects that we over-identify ourselves with it and human resources professionals and leaders try to formulate policies and activities towards that goal but we should always be consciously aware of our limits of doing so.

Being consciously aware of answers to some questions might bring more clarity and awareness for us. Are we sure we will be working with the same organization or place or with same colleagues five years from now? How many colleagues from our last organization or work location are still our friends? Is our organization as passionate about us as we are about our organization and if yes, will this passion continue once we move-out? Will a colleague or team-member or manager whom we consider friend or guide reciprocate our gestures of sacrifice or over-enthusiasm?

We must be consciously aware that change is part of work life. Organizations, geography, teams, roles keep changing and too much sense of belongingness might impact our sense of judgment or decision-making and acceptance of and adaptation to change.

The above conscious self-awareness about social needs doesn't imply we should be socially detached in our work life. It implies that a balance is always required when it comes to meeting social needs because over-emphasizing social-life at work-place at the cost of own personal and social relations may result in emotional trauma when there is change of job, work-place or organization.

Esteem Needs

Maslow had classified esteem needs into two types i.e. the desire for reputation or respect from others (status, prestige) and esteem for oneself (dignity, achievement, mastery, independence). In corporate context, esteem needs occupy a prominent place and the classification given by Maslow, holds true in work life context too.

Desire for respect from others i.e. prestige or status

In work life or work-place setting and also in our personal life, a lot of dissonance happens due to this esteem need. Let us analyse what role does the motivation related to prestige or status need play in our life. A few keen observations or questions can help us as a guide. Are we over-emphasizing our identification with organization in front of our personal and social circle? Have we made it a prestige issue? It happens a lot with professionals working in well-known brands. Such professionals become prisoners of that motivational need and their decision-making gets impacted.

At a personal level, we tend to over-emphasize this need through demanding and enjoying hierarchy related power and prestige. Once we move out from that hierarchy or role through change of job, place or organization, we feel lot of distress and unhappiness.

We must be consciously aware of and avoid this need in ourselves. We also need to be consciously aware and realize that every job is transitory and it keeps changing. It is always advisable to keep personal and professional life separate.

Esteem for oneself

As human beings, need for dignity, achievement and independence is inherent. However, the priority of this need and consequent intensity of motivation differ from one professional to another.

Are the parameters of personal dignity, achievement and independence important to us in our corporate life and affect our decision-making? When our manager admonishes us publicly, does it really upset us and do we wish we could change our job? Are we achievement-oriented, feel internally satisfied when we achieve our targets, praised for the same and prefer roles where we can make visible contribution? Do we prefer roles where we get a lot of independence compared to roles where we are micro-managed?

If our response is in the affirmative for the above, then the esteem for oneself and related motivation is high in our priority and it does matter to us.

Self-Actualization

Self-actualization needs involve realizing personal potential, self-fulfilment and seeking personal growth. A desire "to become everything one is capable of becoming." (Maslow, 1987, p.64)

In work life, we find lot of people trying to meet this need, sometimes even at the cost of other basic needs. Whether we give priority to this motivational need reflects in our behaviours such as trying new ideas or plans instead of sticking to the old ones, giving importance to our feelings in evaluating events or situations instead of blindly following or believing people in authority or in majority, looking at life objectively and avoiding office politics and being honest. More related behaviours are - being prepared to be unpopular even if our ideas or views don't coincide with majority or people in authority; taking responsibility and working hard to achieve goals, accepting ourselves and others as they are; trying to identify our weaknesses and courage to accept the same and work towards improvement; emphasizing democratic attitude; and having strong moral and ethical standards.

Self-actualization is a matter of degree and exists in varying degrees in a few of us who feel the need for self-actualization and such behaviours motivate us. It involves the quest for realizing our complete potential. Such behaviours can also lead to a lot of dissonance because some colleagues or managers of ours may not prefer us indulging in such behaviours and either out of competition or jealousy or they may not have understanding of this need and its related behaviours.

*

Maslow (1987) had pointed-out that most behaviour is multi-motivated and noted that "any behaviour tends to be determined by several or all of the basic needs simultaneously rather than by only one of them." This holds true for us in work-life. However, reaching a state of self-actualization as well as materialistic growth, prestige and status are necessary. So are physiological, safety and social needs. But, proper ordering of our needs is also essential. Most of the times, we mistake all our needs as necessities. A true conscious self-awareness will limit our needs reasonably. This, limiting of needs reasonably, will positively impact our professional life through conscious actions and behaviours.

Let us remember when we took-up our job, we wanted a good salaried job or in some cases just a job and salary was our happiness destination. When we got that, we became happy. Now lets us start becoming aware of our happiness from here. If we got the job in less efforts, we start thinking, I wish I had tried harder and maybe I would have got a better job. Where is the happiness destination? This was first shifting of happiness destination. Then, we compare ourselves with our class-mates or colleagues and we find that some of them are better than us in salary or designation or brand of organization and we become unhappy. This is second shifting of happiness destination. Subsequently, as we move forward we look for higher salaries, bigger house and car year-after year and if we don't get the same, we again become unhappy. Why this unhappiness? We need to be consciously aware that it happens because we have been considering happiness as a destination and making it dependent on external factors.

A consciously aware seeking of happiness doesn't exclude the materialistic aspects of life but enables us to be consciously aware that these are just means of living our life and not entire life itself. It enables us to understand the real necessity of each materialistic desire and give it only that much importance which it deserves in our life.

A lot of times, over-emphasizing one need at the cost of another basic need may lead to behaviours with consequences, which adversely affect the under-emphasized basic need. For example, over-emphasizing independence need and resulting persistent behaviour of seeking an independent role may result in adverse effect on job security, thereby inadvertently under-emphasizing economic security need. This is the reason, we must always be consciously aware of 'what matters to us' and our priority of needs and behave accordingly. Similarly, if we over-emphasizes esteem need and reacts every time with extreme behaviours for every contradicting professional view, then we will find ourselves in dissonance with almost everyone leading to lot of unhappiness for us and also for others.

Though, all or some of the needs may be simultaneously affecting our behaviour yet, for each of us the priority of needs will vary and that priority guides our professional behaviour. A conscious self-awareness of our priority of needs i.e. 'what actually matters' will help us organize our actions, behaviour, activities, and decisions accordingly. This will further bring inner peace and outer harmony and synergy leading to a state of happiness for us.

Priority of Ethical and Moral Standards

Our moral and ethical standards are more at a subconscious level and become visible in our behaviours during a dilemma involving moral and ethical values. As different professionals, each of us accord different priority to ethics, honesty, integrity, truthfulness, and justice etc. This priority results from our upbringing and effect of role models in our early life.

This factor has a major bearing on our synergy or dissonance in the work place as different professionals and organizations accord varying priority to this important facet. A lot of times, we behave and take decisions as per our moral and ethical values irrespective of other factors at play and this causes dissonance. As professionals, we must be consciously aware of our values and the priority we wish to accord to these important parts of our personality. However, in spite of being consciously self-aware, effecting changes in the surrounding environment may not be possible but being consciously aware of our surrounding certainly helps us in better understanding, accepting and adapting to our surrounding environment.

Our moral and ethical values are the strongest pillars of our personality and any dissonance of our values with our colleagues or organizational values and culture results in dilemmas and inner turmoil and consequent loss of peace of mind. This contributes to unhappiness for us. Those people who follow higher levels of ethical and moral values are generally more contended and happy than those who attach their happiness to materialistic acquisitions and are always shifting their happiness destinations once they achieve what they previously desired.

"A person who is aware of himself is in a better position to predict and control his own behaviour." – B.F.Skinner

For us, being consciously self-aware implies knowing, understanding and being consciously aware of our inner feelings at conscious, subconscious or unconscious levels of what really matters in life, priority of our motivational needs in work life and the priority we accord to ethical and moral values. Being consciously self-aware, we are in a better position to determine our happiness through bringing harmony and synergy between our inner-self and outer behaviours. It also enables us being more acceptable of other's behaviours because we become conscious that similar to our stage of not being consciously self-aware, others may also be feeling dissonance between their inner-self and outer behaviours. A conscious acceptance of other's behaviours leads to inner peace and happiness.

After we have become consciously self-aware, which is more at an inner level, the next step in the conscious awareness journey is moving to the immediate outer world which includes our and other's personality types and behaviours thereof.

3. I am I, You are you

The only thing that will make us happy is who we are and not who people think we are. Knowing ourselves deeply enough through objectively observing ourselves and once we are aware as to who we are, accepting our reality, irrespective it being good or bad, positive or negative is the first step towards bringing synergy in our inner-self. We must accept who we are because finding happiness without accepting, who we actually are, may not be possible. We must know and accept that each one of us is born unique so there is no use trying to be someone else or not knowing or accepting who we are. We have a personality which has been shaped by our heredity and environment and that unique combination makes us unique.

Each one of us is unique and has a unique personality of our, which differentiates us from others. Personality is the sum total of a person's feelings, thoughts and needs expressed in behaviour patterns. A conscious awareness of various personality types existing in work place enables us to understand how we and others, as professionals, are likely to behave or act while interacting in different situations.

Different types of individuals have been psychologically classified as Personality Types, with either different purpose or different parameters of the classification. One example of type theory is Type A and Type B Personality Theory. According to this theory, Type A individuals are more competitive, highly organized, ambitious, impatient and aggressive, whereas Type B are more relaxed, easy-going, less neurotic, patient and explainable people. The theory originally suggested that Type A individuals were more prone to developing coronary heart diseases, though it wasn't empirically proved.

Another important and widely used classification, Sixteen Personality Factor Questionnaire (16PF), was developed after several decades of empirical research by Raymond B. Cattell, Maurice Tatsuoka and Herbert Eber. It provides clinicians with a normal range of measurement of anxiety, adjustment, emotional stability and behavioural problems. These 16 factors or some of these factors have also been used in corporate world for various purposes such as Career Development Report, Occupational Selection, Teamwork Development Report, Management Potential Report and Leadership Coaching Report etc.

However, these typologies are used either by clinicians or by psychologists or by trained human resources professionals. Dividing personalities based on psychological or sociological types, for which plenty of information is already available, has remained more academic in nature as well as psychologically or sociologically contextual. Working professionals, with exception of a few Human resources department professionals, rarely try to understand or relate to these academic personality types. For us, as common professionals, these typologies don't make much sense.

We all have heard acronyms for various professionals including ourselves and the most common terms used in work life are generalized stereotypes such as 'autocratic, democratic, good or bad' being used for manager, 'nice human being', 'loyal', 'honest', 'hard-working' or some slangs used for unethical, immoral or bad colleagues.

In work-place setting, effective typologies need to be simple and must allow for increased ability to understand behaviour of colleagues, teams, managers, or leaders in work-place setting. These typologies must help us develop effective strategies for moulding our behaviour to bring more harmony, which can help us in being more professionally productive and personally satisfying.

Let us focus on two words i.e. 'we' and 'objectively'. Why these two words only? As professionals, finding out 'who we are' in an 'objective way' will help us assess our strengths, weaknesses and situations where we have higher probability of synergies and where there is likely to be dissonance. Similarly, objectively assessing and analysing behaviour traits of our colleagues, including teams we are managing and seniors we are interacting with, will help us gain an understanding about our position relative to our colleagues, and if there are synergies or dissonances and why so. This will further help us in making decisions in the short-term as well as long-term and save us of many dilemmas that we face on day-to-day basis.

Let us try and understand Personalities and corresponding behaviour traits of ours in a working set-up. From professional's perspective, the more relevant and important aspects to know, understand and become aware of include what we bring on table with respect to contribution, behaviours in work-setting and priority we accord to ethical and moral values. These aspects contribute majorly while defining the work-personality of each one of us. The words we are using to describe each personality type aren't meant to label people but are more relatable in a work-place context and allows for increased ability to understand behaviours.

Hercules Personality

According to Greek or Roman mythology, Hercules is a hero of superhuman strength and courage who performed twelve immense tasks imposed on him and who after death was ranked among the Gods. So, as the name suggests, the Herculean personality type people have immense energy & power and can pull the entire train i.e. a team of junior or middle-managers by themselves.

In work-place setting, we can be looked at as Hercules Personality professionals if we are very hard working, tenacious, highly ethical and believe everything can be achieved with hard work, sincere effort and strength or all of them combined. Hercules professionals are highly emotional and tend to express their emotions openly. This emotional trait generally proves to be our biggest weakness in a corporate or even in a social set-up.

With Hercules traits, we are respected and regarded very highly as colleagues and leaders among our teams. Such personality makes us the best fit for being part of a team or leading very well defined tasks i.e. projects or heading operational teams requiring immense efforts. In ambiguous tasks, we tend to perform best under guidance.

Aristotle Personality

Aristotle was a Greek philosopher who made significant and lasting contributions to nearly every aspect of human knowledge, from logic to biology to ethics and aesthetics. In Arabic philosophy, he was known as 'The First Teacher' and in the West, he was 'The Philosopher'. Even today, Aristotle's work remains a significant starting point for any argument in the fields of logic, aesthetics, political theory and ethics.

As the name suggests, The Aristotle personality professionals have immense knowledge on every aspect of the business and much more. If we compare a herculean professionals to the arms or muscles in our body, then Aristotle professionals are the brains of our body. If we have Aristotle personality traits, we are good at providing strategy, mentoring and guiding and are suitable for strategizing, providing leadership at highest levels where we should generally take the backseat after providing a direction and let herculean personality types execute the strategy.

However, if we show Aristotle personality traits at junior or mid-level in individual contributor or team-member roles, we can be perceived as a big drag on the team. Our team-members may get a feeling that we do nothing except trying to tell what to do. In that case, as Aristotle professionals, we are more suited for consultancy jobs.

Can a driver take a train to its destination if there is no engine in the train? Similarly, in leadership or managerial roles, as Aristotle professionals, we can be highly successful if we have herculean professionals to support us in executing our thoughts and strategies else we might fail miserably.

Professor Personality

Literally, the word 'professor' derives from Latin as a "person who professes" being usually an expert in arts or sciences, a teacher of the highest rank. In a work-place setting, a few of us can be described as the 'Professor Personality' type if we have views on everything, express our views without much thinking, consider ourselves to be omniscient, speak a lot and are opinion-makers and sometimes even act as trouble-shooters for management. We can either be very suave and polished or simply irritating full of 'I, me, myself' attitude and criticizing everything, overtly or covertly.

> *Subroto is neither a good listener nor good at keeping secrets and information gets shared even without him being aware that he has shared a confidential information. He brings a lot of negativity in the team through his constant gossips and views and has sometimes proved to be very costly by spoiling customer relationships. As a manager, he wastes a lot of time in meetings or conference halls with little positive outcome, as the communication is generally one way boastful narration. His team dread the idea of attending his meetings and always try to avoid him.*

Those of us with Professor Personality type, who are suave and polished ones add a lot of value when put in customer-facing roles such as sales or commercial or customer relationship management roles. In these roles, we can be a big asset to the organization.

As colleagues of such professionals, we must avoid talking informal things or expressing opinions about other colleagues, senior management or company. As a manager of such professionals, we must endeavour to move them into customer-facing roles and advise them to be good listeners.

Passenger Personality

A passenger is someone who is traveling in the vehicle by paying for the travel and enjoying or bearing with the ride but not driving or operating the vehicle. In a work set-up, some of us can be described as Passengers Personality professionals if we perform our tasks as a routine and deliver as per expectations from our respective roles. We tend not to take any initiative for additional tasks or roles but are happy to come to office on time, finish our task and go back on time. For us, a job is just a job where we work to earn livelihood for our family similar to a passenger in a cab who takes the cab to reach a destination and pays for his ride.

As professionals, we don't indulge in extra ego messaging of our managers and don't want to indulge in office politics. With these traits, we are neither highly visible ones nor someone who can be pointed-out as non-performer. Looking more positively, we are similar to the foot soldiers of an army. Just as an Army needs whole lot of foot soldiers, a working set-up or company needs lot of people to do routine jobs. These jobs as well as such employees are important, as such jobs need to be done on a daily basis to run day-to-day operations.

> *Henry described one of his team-mates Hemant, who has Passenger Personality, as: "Hemant isn't highly ambitious and it is easier to motivate him. He doesn't have specific career goals and can jump the ship as soon as he gets a better salary somewhere else. The best part is - it is easier to find his substitute. What I like about him is that he doesn't indulge in office politics and whatever is told to him, he will do that work, irrespective of results. I have advised him to be careful and that he should neither get stuck at one place for a very long time nor become very complacent in the process."*

As Passenger personality professionals, work-life balance is more important for us and we prioritize taking care of our family by not over-focusing on our work-place. We aren't highly conscious of ethical or compliance related matters in work-life and generally do as directed by our managers.

In a leadership or managerial role, we need to keep our work-force motivated and this group i.e. the 'Passenger personality type' forms majority of our work-force so we must make sure to keep them motivated. Our empathetic behaviour towards them is their biggest motivator.

Free Rider Personality

Free Rider is someone who enjoys a benefit accruing from a collective effort, but contributes little or nothing to the effort. In a work set-up too, Free Rider Personality professionals are the ones who don't contribute anything to the team-efforts or company goals but they get equal benefits, salaries and bonuses.

In work-setting, some of us may be displaying Free Rider Personality behaviours wherein we don't contribute anything in the tasks assigned to us or to our teams and prefer to take-up team tasks instead of individual tasks. Within team tasks, we will prefer to be seen with team-members who are contributing more than others so that our non-contribution isn't visible to others. Apart from not contributing to the team effort, we also indulge in ego messaging by showering compliments on, eulogizing and glorifying their managers or important stakeholders to divert attention from our non-contribution.

Being such professionals, we prefer to work in ambiguous situations and tasks where no individual responsibility can be fixed. With time, our team-members realize our non-contribution and therefore we tend to have poor relationships with our team-members. If a team task is heading for failure, being free riders, we try to move-out of the task even before the task is over. We aren't concerned much with ethical or compliance related matters in the work-place.

As managers of such personality type team-members, we must be conscious of the fact that there may either be temporary free riders or habitual ones and we need to distinguish between the two. The temporary free riders may have become free riders due to either a feeling that the task is useless with no gains for them or company; or no clarity on 'why' of a task; or roles being not very well defined and ambiguity about their own required contribution; or when they find that the team size is too big and it is impossible to see who is doing what; or poor team relationships. As soon as we, as managers, take care of above or similar reasons, lot of temporary ones become effective contributors and the productivity levels rise. The habitual free riders are the ones who need to be found-out and got rid of on priority basis. They are not only the dead wood but also free riding is contagious wherein their colleagues might feel that if so and so is free riding, why not me.

Hypocrite Personality

The word 'hypocrite' came into English language from the Greek word *hypokrites* which means 'an actor' or 'a stage player'. In the Bible, hypocrite refers to a person who pretends to have moral, virtues, religious beliefs or principles; that he or she doesn't actually possess, especially a person who actions belie his stated beliefs. Similar to the word origin and its use in religious literature, the word hypocrite is quite often used in the corporate world too. It is used to refer to those professionals who claim to have and follow highest standards of values, morals, ethics and corporate governance but their actions contradict their claim or stated position.

Irrespective of the fact that we may or may not be aware, some of us may be exhibiting Hypocrite Personality type if we always take high moral ground during conversations and discussions on topics such as following ethical principles, doing justice at all times, presenting a holier than cow image of ourselves; but in reality we don't practice what we preach whether it is corporate governance or ethics and values. Instead, we circumvent the rules through either reading or quoting the rules as it suits us or making others circumvent the same pretending as if that particular rule is a minor issue.

> *Asit seemed to be very humble and friendly. He was generally suave, good actor and easily earned sympathies of his colleagues by presenting a 'bechara' (i.e. simple, helpless, harmless) image of himself. However, he followed double standards i.e. one set of values, morals or ethics for himself and in situations which might affect him and another set of values, morals or ethics for others or situations involving team-members or colleagues. He was perceived to be simple and harmless because of his zero reactions towards people or situations, in which a normal person might feel slighted or ego-hurt and therefore may react somewhat. Actually, he was too egoistic but, being very good actor, he could show as if nothing has happened. He could keep his feelings hidden, for long periods of time, till he was in a situation when he could take revenge. In the process of seeking revenge, he could go to any extent such as sabotaging careers of colleagues or team-members through well-planned conspiracy.*

Professionals with hypocrite personality traits in managerial or leadership roles can cause maximum harm to their colleagues or their team-members and that too without anyone knowing the same.

Mercenary Personality

Origin of the word mercenary is from Latin word '*mercenarius*' meaning 'one who does anything for pay'. Most dictionaries define a mercenary as professionals soldier hired to serve in a foreign army with a primary motivation of personal gain at the expense of ethics. Similar to its literal meaning, in corporate world or work set-up too, the Mercenary professionals are the ones who tend to make or help to make maximum profits, for the company or the organization they work for, overlooking values, ethics, corporate governance policies and laws of the land.

The infamous 'Enron Scandal' was one such case where people in Enron management, including their CEO, who were responsible for the scandal, fit very easily into the Mercenary Personality type. In case of Enron, the scale of fraud, fudging of financial data and conspiracy was very big. But the same might have happened or still happening at a smaller scale at various places in corporate world or smaller work-places and people with the mercenary personality traits are the ones who would be either planning or executing the same with majority in their organizations being oblivious of their nefarious designs. It is very dangerous to work for or work with such personality types.

How do we find-out the mercenary personality type in a work-place setting? Such professionals carry an aura around themselves or their roles as if they are doing some heavenly task and give extraordinary business results year-after-year in spite of business environment being not so conducive at times. Such professionals avoid corporate governance, values or ethics in the garb of so-called greater good of the entire team and business. They pretend to be following a higher set of values and ethics which transcend everything else.

We must be aware that unlike a mercenary soldiers, the mercenary personality professionals in work-setting, talk a lot, often taking their skills to demagogic levels and aren't good listeners. Such people aren't transparent in true sense though they pretend to be highly transparent. Anyone asking uncomfortable questions, regarding them not following some compliances or laws of the land, is either snubbed or completely side-lined by them.

Mercenary professionals always have a small coterie of professionals who form an inner group and executes key strategic decisions with, sometimes, a wall of secrecy surrounding the role and working of this group. In an extreme situations, they create an environment where, everyone feels the highest level mercenary in that group of mercenary personality type is the fountainhead of all power and he is eulogized and kind of worshipped. This creates a halo effect for him and majority professionals in the organization stop questioning their decision-making and follow them blindly.

We, as their team-member or manager, need to be highly conscious and cautious of such personality types. These are the professionals who not only harm by being faulty role models to their juniors but also resulting in cases such Enron at similar or smaller levels. Mercenary professionals can sometimes be misjudged as Hercules by their extra energy and result-orientation.

Parasite Personality

Word origin of parasite is from Greek '*parasitos*' meaning one who lives at another's expense. The business dictionary defines 'parasite' as an organism obtaining nourishment from or living on another organism (the 'host') for survival and usually harming it and causing disease. Some parasites are partly independent and some depend entirely on their hosts and separate only when either one of them dies. Also, scientists have uncovered many parasite-host relationships in which the parasite actually alters the brain and behaviour of its host to make it assist in fulfilling vital parts of the parasite's life cycle.

In work-place setting, we can always find such professionals who are not contributing in the team-effort but are always found at the right time and place in order to take the credit for other's hard work. Sometimes they even manage to show that they are the ones who did everything. These professionals indulging in immense flattery, eulogizing and excessively complimenting their managers or colleagues whom they are using or plan to use as host.

> *Sen's sudden visibility at the new project site headed by Rahul had become too noticeable. They both were senior level colleagues but everyone was wondering why Sen had become so regular at this site while it is getting completed. He had no role to play here and had not contributed anything in the project. However, he was certainly visible when Raman, their MD, visited project site. Singh was habitual of ego messaging Raman by showering compliments, eulogizing and glorifying him though on his back, he excessively criticized Raman too.*
>
> *Rahul and even his team could see through it but everyone kept quiet and focused on completing the project. Rahul even knew that Sen was talking about him to Raman very negatively. But did Raman realize all this or was he promoting such behavior of Sen as part of his own office politics?*

If they are using us as host, they manage to alter our (the host) behaviour with others by constantly feeding us with wrong information. They project their negative behaviours on us (the host) and make us and others believe that we are the bad ones whereas they are the good ones. Such personality type not only lack compassion for our feelings but also always project themselves as the victims, the hurt ones or needy. We (the host) always find ourselves placating this personality type or sympathizing with them because of the illusion they might have created about themselves in our mind. In the process, the negativity, which ideally should have been towards them, starts shifting towards us.

*

Having understood the above eight personality types, it is important for us to note here that we will certainly not always be displaying behavioural traits of one personality or another but it will be a mix and will also depend on situations as well as hierarchical levels. However, when we exhibit majority of traits from one personality and a smaller mix of other personalities, we can be safely assumed to belong to the personality exhibiting maximum traits of one or two personalities.

Though, we, as professionals, can display behaviours of two or three personality, yet a few personality traits can never occur simultaneously in any single professional because of their contradictory or opposite nature.

A Hercules professional can never be a Mercenary because if we look deeper into the two, a Mercenary is opposite of Hercules in more than one ways, such as Hercules professional is highly ethical and morally upright whereas a

Mercenary isn't. The later seems to be following his/her own different set of moral principles. Similarly, Hercules doesn't follow a leader or manager blindly whereas a Mercenary does. A Hercules delivers results within legal boundaries whereas a Mercenary delivers results irrespective of legal compliances. Hercules believes in growth of its team members along with himself whereas Mercenary believes in his own growth only. A Hercules takes responsibility for failures but a Mercenary blames others or team for failures.

Similarly, a Hercules professional can't be a Hypocrite, Free Rider or Parasite. He can certainly display traits of Aristotle, Professor or Passenger in varying degrees. An Aristotle professional owing to his higher thought development and understanding can never be a Mercenary because unlike a Mercenary, he understands impact of not following legal compliances or blindly following a manager. Similarly, Aristotle professional can never display traits of be a Parasite type because the former understands the futility of the parasitic nature and also because he/she has a lot to offer in terms of planning, strategy, mentoring etc.

A Passenger is never a Free Rider, though it might seem so to someone who isn't a keen observer. A Passenger always completes the assigned task or contributes as per expectations, though he doesn't believe in taking extra initiative or additional roles whereas a Free Rider never or rarely contributes anything at all. The former doesn't indulge in extra ego messaging of his manager whereas the later often does so to hide his non-contribution. A Passenger accepts tasks irrespective of these being individual or team tasks whereas the later always prefers team tasks.

Similarly, a Mercenary professional can never be a Free Rider because the former is hard-working and always delivers, more than expected, on the assigned tasks whereas the later never contributes anything. Mercenary can certainly display traits of a Parasite type along with mercenary traits.

*

As a next step, we need to be very keen observers and very objectively assess ourselves and others on each of the personality. Preferably, top two or three personality behavioural traits must be focused on while assessing ourselves or others because the rest of the behaviours will rarely be noticeable and even if they do, the same will depend on specific situations. This can certainly help us as one of the important tools for decision-making in work-setting. The aim of above is not to categorize people or create stereotypes but to understand and be consciously aware of behaviour patterns exhibited by us and others as employees in corporate setting.

We also need to understand and be consciously aware that an individual can be a very obedient son, loyal and caring husband and ideal father yet a hypocrite and parasite in work-setting. This happens because family and corporate work-setting are two completely different environments and therefore the behaviour traits exhibited or displayed by the same individual at these two different places can be very different.

A conscious self-awareness, regarding our and other's Personality and behaviours in the work life helps us understand reasons of why people behave in a certain manner. It also helps us make conscientious decisions in work as well as personal life. Each personality has developed over a period of time and comes with different priorities and motivational needs in life.

We can never attain happiness if we want everything to be and happen as per our terms and for our limited purposes. For reaching a state and feeling of continued happiness, we must understand and be conscious that just as we want to be accepted as we are, we must accept others as they are. If we want others to be understanding us and adaptive towards us, we need to do the same for others i.e. we also need to understand others and be adaptive and accommodating towards them. Can we direct others to understand us, accept us and be adaptive towards us? Probably not but our understanding, acceptance and adaptation is within our control and that is what we need to start doing to begin with for our inner peace and harmony.

A conscious awareness of this aspect in interpersonal dynamics in work place helps us develop understanding and compassion for other's behaviours and changing our behaviour, wherever required. This can prove to be a major source of happiness through inner peace, harmony and outer synergy. We can use this knowledge of work personality types in a positive ways for understanding and accepting ourselves, as we are and others, as they are.

To be happy, we shouldn't be judgemental of others but be conscious of their motivations, behaviours and personalities to get a better understanding of why people behave the way they do. Being judgemental and using this knowledge to label people will always bring more dissonance and resulting unhappiness for us and for others.

4. Concentric Circles

We all have individual preferences regarding working in certain corporate set-up i.e. some of us prefer and are happy to be working in corporate offices while others are happy to and prefer working in field. Does our initial corporate environment affect these preferences and do we, with differing preferences for working in different work-places, display different behaviours in work-life?

One of the factors affecting happiness at work place is location of the work-place and here we aren't referring to the geographical location but location in relation to the organizational structure. Though, we, as human being, are good at adapting yet we feel the happiest when we are in a place similar to and familiar with the one we are used to be living in or working at.

When we enter work-life, we come with some career goals, expectations, own personality, educational qualifications etc. and then our initial corporate environment, colleagues, leaders, managers, role models that we find in that environment have major impact on our professional personality or our work personality as professionals. Understanding the impact of this initial environment on our work personality not only makes us consciously aware of our behaviours but also makes us realize the importance we play as role models for those professionals who enter the corporate life.

The word 'concentric circles' is used in mathematics to denote circles with common center where the outer circle subsumes the inner circle into it. This metaphor of concentric circles can also be used in the work-life context to understand professional behaviour patterns.

This analysis or the concept of corporate concentric circles isn't meant to create stereotypes among professionals. It is meant to make us understand our and colleague's behaviours in the work-place context. The knowledge, so gained, can help us create more mindful behaviour, which might help us in surviving the corporate maze or mastering the art of survival and growth. It can also help in creating a mental and behavioural balance in the corporate chaos surrounding us.

Using the metaphor of concentric circles in work-place or organizational management structure, let us assume there is generally a central circle comprising of CEO, supported by functional heads, working out of a corporate office. Then there are businesses being managed by the CEO and his team of functional professionals and those are outside this office, either in same building, in different buildings in same city, in different geographies of same country or businesses spread across countries being headed by respective country heads.

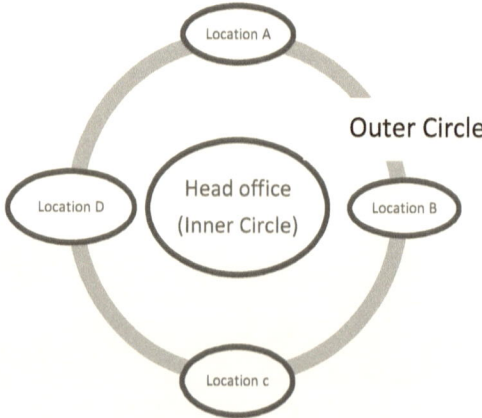

These outer locations or businesses are similar to the outer circle of the two concentric circles. So, a small business might have two concentric circles whereas a multi-national business might be seen as three or more circles with intermediate offices between corporate office and place where actual operations happen.

Let us look at it historically. There used to be a King's court consisting of a King and his ministers who used to be people with specialized knowledge of leading an army, religion, intelligence, administration etc.; on the other hand, there used to be feudal lords under the king who always remained away from the court. It can always be depicted as two or three concentric circles depending the geographical size of the kingdom.

The work personalities of people working in different circles used to be different. The former, i.e. those working in king's court, enjoyed the clout of the king's court, drew power from their position in the court itself and rarely hesitated in being total yes-men to the King. The later, i.e. those working as feudal lords, enjoyed the independence and free-hand that they got while being feudal lords, with almost being in a position similar to the king, though on a smaller scale.

In a federal republic such as India, this metaphor can be seen, though with reduced intensity, in the context of Union cabinet in the central government and Chief Ministers in the state governments.

If we observes keenly, it is easy to find that most of the times in work-life too, some of us fit more in the inner-most circle which entails a corporate role i.e. as functional heads in the office of managing director; whereas there is rest of us are usually more happy and productive working at field level i.e.

closer to where actual business happens, which forms the outer circle in corporate concentric circles. It holds true for bureaucratic set-up too.

A lot of times, we wonder as to why a particular professional has always been working in head office while another one is always in a field office or heading business away from head office. If such individuals change their place of work from head-office to field or vice-versa, there is dissonance for the professional and also for the teams. A lot of times, we hear our colleagues commenting – why so and so has been sent to field, he was more suited for head office and vice-versa.

Are there only temporary behavioural differences or major personality type differences among people working in different concentric circles of an organization, if yes, why is it so. A good start to this might be closely and keenly observing people working in two different set-ups in our organization. We can keenly observe these behavioural differences and with few exceptions, find some prominent behavioural traits for the inner circle i.e. head office professionals and for the outer circle i.e. field professionals.

Inner Concentric Circle

Those of us who are viewed as and are comfortable working in the Inner Concentric Circle are more agreeable to authority or people in power, draw our authority from the leader's position of power in the hierarchy and we prefer to keep quiet and don't speak our mind, if we find that our idea doesn't match leader's idea. We tend to be submissive in corporate office yet very authoritative towards people in field and always prefer our word to be the final one.

We tend to be good at managing or navigating through office politics, suave, diplomatic and polished in our behaviours and communication whereas our man-management or team-management skills may not be so good. We avoid taking ownership or responsibility but always take accolades for every success, even when the success might have been achieved by the team working in field without any contribution from the inner circle i.e. corporate office.

Owing to our closeness to the leader, we are good at building perception of others, suiting our needs and goals and due to the aura of the corporate office, as inner circle professionals, we tend to have a false feeling of superiority over our colleagues working in the field, who are doing actual business.

We prefer and feel happy taking specialized functional roles such as finance, marketing, HR, IT, Admin etc. even if asked to move to the field and are good at creating corporate policy documents and desk-work.

Outer Concentric Circle

Those of us who prefer and are comfortable working in the Outer Concentric Circle, or place where actual business operations happen, tend to display independent thought process and working style and don't prefer to be micro-managed or guided at every step. We are generally outspoken and upfront and express our opinion even if our opinion differs from leader's opinion. We generally possess good man-management and team-management skills but are not good at office politics and navigating through the same.

We get motivation out of actual business-related work and likes to be openly appreciated. We take ownership and responsibility and are more suited for team-facing or customer-centric roles such as operations, sales or actual leadership roles because we believe we possess actual business or related work-area knowledge instead of literary knowledge.

There might be exceptions to the above described behaviour patterns of professionals belonging to either of the concentric circles, based on specific personalities as discussed in the section on various personality types. Similarly, there may be a head office at the centre with four locations which further have a smaller version of head-offices with actual operations happening in the plant or area of operation. So, each setting has to be seen in actual structural context.

Heredity and Environment in work-place context

Now the question arises as to why there are differences in behaviour patterns of professionals working in separate concentric circle work-settings. Effects of heredity and environment on personality development of an individual is a widely researched, read and discussed topic in psychological studies. An individual's personality is the product of both heredity and environment. Though, behaviour patterns shown by us as professionals are also affected by heredity and environmental factors but the same need to be looked at from a slightly different perspective on heredity and environment.

Biologically speaking, heredity is what is inherited as genes from our parents and in psychology terms, environment is a sum total of the social environment we get after birth. Both these factors play their respective roles in our personality development.

Our personality has developed by the time we enter professional life, yet our professional or work personality and behaviour patterns are yet to take shape. There are two very important factors which affect the emergence or making of our work personality. First factor is - the already developed personality and the professional degree with which we enter the work-life and this can be equated to the heredity factor of the psychology studies. We can't change it once we have entered work-life. Second factor is similar to environmental factor discussed earlier in psychology parlance, with the only difference being that here environment refers to the work-place and work-culture where we spend initial years of our work-life journey.

If maximum of this time is spent in the inner concentric circle environment then our work personality development, ease of working and happiness which we get working at a particular place will be more inclined toward corporate office working. Whereas, if our maximum time is spent in the outer concentric circle i.e. in the field, closer to the actual business operations, then our work personality will be more independent natured and our inclination will be towards working more in field roles and we will feel happy working in such environment.

Now if we enter the work-life with a functional specialization such as HR, Marketing or Strategy, then working in a work set-up throughout our professional life is a given. On the other hand, if we have entered through engineering or operations degree, then usually that professional gets field roles which are the places where actual business happens.

In either case, we, as new entrants, come in contact with leaders, colleagues and related work-culture. We start perceiving organization from that very circle's perspective and get used to working in that particular culture type. Even without consciously trying, we acquire or emulate behaviour patterns of our immediate leaders and colleagues with whom we spend lot of our initial professional time.

Two young professionals Dave and Himesh enter the same organization with same degree but in different concentric circles.

Dave was assigned a role in the outer concentric circle i.e. on the shop-floor of manufacturing plant. He saw people actually making things happen on ground, taking ownership or responsibility of a task and enjoying the same after completing the task, discussing things openly. His personality gets impacted by these actions of others which is the work environment and he too starts doing the same. These behaviours become a habit over a period of time and start reflecting in usual behaviour patterns of Dave, even without his conscious knowledge.

Himesh was a young entrant with similar professional degree as that of Dave but assigned a role in inner concentric circle i.e. corporate office of the manufacturing unit. He saw colleagues being diplomatic, not so open or straight-forward in their communications, agreeing to the leader of the inner circle almost on all occasions and trying to throw their weight around when dealing with shop-floor employees or supervisors of the manufacturing plant. Himesh too started emulating these actions and these very actions become habits and his displayed behaviour patterns over a period of time.

As consciously aware professionals, we must always take into account the impact of initial work environment on development of our and other's work personality. To know, understand and become aware of the effect of priorities of life, priority of motivational needs, individual's motivational needs and initial work environment on our and colleague's personality type and behaviours, helps us improve our conscious awareness. It also makes us aware of the probable reasons of our preference for a particular role in inner or outer concentric circle and our responsibility in wholesome development of ourselves and our junior professionals when they enter corporate world.

This conscious awareness leads to better understanding and acceptance of our and other's behaviours and preferences related to work-place. This understanding and acceptance brings inner and outer synergy and consequent happiness for us as well as for others.

Having gained conscious awareness of our and other's personalities in work-life context, related behaviours and impact of initial work environment on work-personality development, we are ready to move into the realm of interpersonal dynamics of various personalities. When we, as professionals with varying personalities, interact in any work-setting, the result can be either complete synergy or complete dissonance or something in between these two extremes. As emphasized earlier, synergy or dissonance are major factors impacting our happiness at work-place and therefore we need to be consciously aware of our synergies as well as dissonances.

5. Synergy or Dissonance

"Synergy is better than my way or your way. It's our way."

–Stephen Covey

In human dynamics, presence of synergy or dissonance between us and others affects our and other's inner peace, happiness and career growth. At the same time, it impacts other stakeholders and team or business or organization we are working with. Happiness isn't about absence of inner and outer differences, dissonances and dilemmas; but it is about being consciously aware of them and reasons thereof, accepting them, dealing with them positively wherever we can and making conscious decisions wherever we know we can't deal with them. Our ability to deal with them comes from our conscious awareness of inherent personality or values or ethics-related fundamental differences between ourselves and others.

In the journey of developing conscious awareness, we must know, understand and be consciously aware of inter-personality dynamics i.e. compatibility or incompatibility among various personalities. It will help us understand as to which personalities will go along well and which ones find difficulties working together. At our work-place, interactions and resulting synergy or dissonance can be at the same levels of hierarchy or across levels because expectations regarding our behaviour greatly depends on roles or hierarchical levels in an organization.

Synergy at Same Levels

At a junior level, our requirements of the job include working at an individual level, but more closely as a team wherein almost everyone in the team is supposed to be enthusiastic, learning quickly on the job, adapting to the new work culture etc. However, the synergy, collaboration and agreements depend a lot on our manager's personality, company culture and type of task etc. In spite of these factors, our individual personalities have a major bearing on the synergy among us as individuals and also at team levels.

At a middle-management level, the requirements of our job change and include equal emphasis on managing a team and working collaboratively with other managers who are also managing their teams. Also, owing to the pyramidal structures of organizations, a sense of some competition with the colleagues sets-in by the time we reach middle management levels and this too has effect on synergies or differences among colleagues at these levels.

At a senior management level, the requirements of the job and expectations from us as managers or leaders change from just delivering on targets to also providing direction and strategy, being a role model, collaborating with other senior leaders and conflict resolution among our team-members. At a sub-conscious level, there is heightened competition with other senior colleagues, as the hierarchical pyramids of workplaces narrow towards the top, which sometimes make even survival as the key consideration for some of us at senior management level. All these factors have positive or negative effects on the behaviours and consequent synergies or dissonances between us as colleagues at these levels.

Also, by the time we reach senior management level, we have already developed a particular work personality or a combination which has been shaped by the knowledge gained so far and various professional environments we have worked in. However, we might have also developed disguise techniques to camouflage our core personality and which would help presenting ourselves as an ideal professional. These techniques would have been learnt either as part of survival techniques or growth strategies used by many of us knowingly or unknowingly. Still, the core personalities don't change and we need to keenly observe ourselves, colleagues and our managers or leaders at senior management level for slightly longer duration to understand our or other's core personalities.

These synergies between personalities will be different at different job levels in the hierarchy of an organization. For example, as a Herculean professional we may not have any synergy and don't want to work with a colleague showing free rider personality in our team while both are at junior-management level. However, the same may not hold true at a senior management level because by that time, in addition to being a Hercules professional, we might have developed some traits of Aristotle personality too or become more mindful in our behaviour. However, the basic synergy or dissonance remains at subconscious level and the only difference is how much we have learnt to adapt to others and to react with lesser intensity or not react at all.

Our knowledge, understanding and conscious awareness regarding synergy or dissonance helps us see the reasons behind behavioural differences existing at surface and subconscious levels. Through this we can always be conscious of the reasons of extreme behaviours of our colleagues and understand why we need not react in every situation.

If we have differences with our colleagues at similar levels and if those differences are visible to our teams, to other colleagues at same level and to senior management, then we can be perceived in poor light, in spite of our target achievement. It may also affect the learning curve of junior management team members of ours because every manager's behaviour and style of working has a great impact on junior professional's learning.

While looking at synergies or dissonances between various professionals at middle or senior level handling teams, we can also observe that the when two professionals have good synergies, their teams will also display good synergies and vice versa. And this is the reason that when we are handling a team comprising of managers or leaders, bringing about synergies in our teams become important for not only their success but our success too. In such situations, instead of looking the other way or brushing conflicts under the carpet, we need to be consciously aware of reasons of conflict, put-in extra efforts, and spend time and energy in conflict resolution among team-leaders.

Synergy between Different Levels

The understanding of synergy or dissonance among various personality types between two professionals while we are interacting from different hierarchical-levels is equally important. When we talk of hierarchical levels, we need to be conscious of the fact that even in matrix organizations, a hierarchy does exist. In fact, it becomes even more complex from our i.e. professional's point-of-view, as the number of important stakeholders, to be managed, increases.

As professionals, our inter-level synergy or dissonance with higher level professionals assumes increased importance in view of the fact that our role allocation and career progression gets immensely impacted by this factor. Also, some organizations, who have matured from human resources perspective, follow 360 degree assessment and in such cases team-members of teams that we manage, also rate us i.e. their next levels and then this very synergy assumes even higher importance, irrespective of levels. Apart from our personality differences, certain factors impact our inter-hierarchy synergy with our colleagues.

Impact of National Culture

National culture of the country or geography, we are working at, has an impact on expectations from our higher or lower levels and thereby impacts synergies.

If a country has been a feudalistic society for most part of its history, then the higher hierarchical level professionals expect a more subdued and compliant behaviour from lower level professionals. Whereas the lower level employees look at the higher professionals as guides or mentors, more knowledgeable and someone who should look-after their lower level employee's welfare and growth. In such cultures, being a lower hierarchy level professional, if we express views or ideas which are contradictory to those of higher level professionals, the same may go against us resulting in dissonance. Such dissonance usually happens when the organization propagates openness about expressing ideas while it is operating in countries which have inherited feudalistic mind-set.

On the other hand, in countries which have been emphasizing democratic principles for a very long time and in turn, individual's capability and individuality, expressing opposing idea by a lower hierarchical level professional isn't considered inappropriate by higher-ups, even at subconscious level. So, such actions don't impact synergy or dissonance much.

In effect, personalities don't take a back-seat but these factors will augment certain personality type behaviour traits and make them more pronounced.

Expectations

Apart from the behaviour traits of individual personalities and similar to what we discussed about expectations from same level colleagues, expectations also play a major role in inter-hierarchy level synergies. For example, at a junior or middle management, we expects middle or senior management level professionals to be fair, transparent and looking-after us i.e. their junior employees through constant guidance and mentoring. Whereas, as senior or middle management professionals, irrespective of personality type, we expect our lower level colleagues to always deliver more than expected, though rarely looking into our contribution.

Humbleness and humility

For every one of us, humbleness and humility are greatest virtues, in every situation or interaction, irrespective of levels. However, these two soft-skills or behavioural traits assume increased importance during inter-hierarchy level interactions. This is so because the interactions are far less at inter-hierarchy level, with rarely any expectations of doing something for the professional at another level. In such situations, the most visible personality traits are our behaviour and soft-skills, with etiquettes displayed by juniors towards their next levels and empathy by senior level professionals towards their junior professionals playing a major role in creating a favourable perception as well as increased synergies when required.

Importance of Manager's perception

A manager plays important role in our synergy with higher levels because whatever views our manager expresses about us to his/her colleagues at same or higher levels, during formal and informal conversations, has a major impact on creating a perception about us as a person and professional. Our synergies or dissonances with our seniors always gets impacted by that perception.

A positive perception, created due to our manager's positive feedback, does help us but it is the negative feedback and perception about which we need to be consciously aware of. The degree of harm is much higher if our manager is trying to create or has created a negative perception about us to his/her colleagues. This is so because this negative perception creates a permanent doubt in the minds of our next hierarchical level managers or leaders and they avoid getting us on-board in their teams or projects, even though we may be the most suitable candidate and willing to switch roles.

The synergies or differences that our manager shares with his/her colleagues i.e. our higher levels always impacts our synergies with them. If our manager is in serious dissonance with a particular colleague at his/her same level, and if we share a good relation with our manager, we can expect a cold shoulder from that senior of ours. On the other hand, if we have dissonance with our manager, then that senior colleague might show some really good synergies with us and in extreme cases, may even utilize our dissonance with our manager to settle his scores with our manager.

We need to be consciously aware of the impact of above mentioned factors in actual work-setting. In addition to the above, professionals with various personality types display varied synergies or dissonances levels while they are interacting with professionals at higher or lower levels.

Personality and Synergy

Our personality impacts our synergies both with our colleagues at same level and across hierarchy levels. When different personalities interact in a work setting, the result can be either complete synergy or complete dissonance or something in between these two extremes. Let us discuss how do our personality impacts our synergy in corporate set-up.

Hercules Personality

At a junior level, as Hercules professionals, we have extreme synergies or extreme dissonance with team members due to our behaviour traits and expectations. We tend to have good or very good synergies with our colleagues having Hercules, mercenary and passenger personality. Whereas, we have very low probability of synergies i.e. high dissonance levels with colleagues displaying hypocrite, free rider and parasite personality. At middle level, we tend to display good synergies with all other personality types except colleagues with Free Rider and Parasite behaviours. At senior level, as Hercules professionals, we display good synergies with other Hercules, Aristotle, Professor and Passenger personality type colleagues at same seniority level, unless we are being led or managed by a manager, who doesn't belong to either of these types. Such managers might create dissonance through their biased behaviours, preferences and expectations etc. We will have low or average synergies with rest of the professionals and our behaviour extremes will depend on how much we have learnt to be less reactive and more mindful in our behaviours.

At inter-level, as Hercules professionals working at junior and middle hierarchy, we are generally favourites of seniors because of our hard-working and passionate nature as well as our value-addition with respect to business goal achievement and desire to learn at every step. On the other hand, as a Hercules professional at senior levels, we tend to display major synergies with Hercules and Passenger juniors and major dissonance with hypocrite, free-rider and parasite personality type juniors.

A Hercules middle or senior level professional displays strong preferences for those who contribute visibly towards business-goal achievement, are ethical in behaviours and always willing to take additional responsibilities or are at least doing their job without indulging in unnecessary office politics.

Aristotle Personality

At a junior level, as Aristotle professionals, we display only average kind of synergies with all team-members except free-rider and parasite types. Our not so-good synergies are owing to the fact that at junior levels, we aren't much liked, and are perceived as those who aren't working hard towards team-goals. Team-members are more likely to perceive us as someone who doesn't want to make action-oriented contributions.

At middle management levels, since we are more thought-oriented and therefore more mindful in our behaviours, we have good synergies with all except colleagues with Free Rider and Parasite behaviours. However, intensity of our behaviours is not as strong as those of Hercules. At senior levels, we have good synergies with other Hercules, Aristotle, Professor and Passenger professionals whereas low synergies with the rest. However, unlike senior Hercules professionals, as senior Aristotle professionals we tend to be less reactive or slightly more adaptive at surface level.

> *Tom was the CEO whom everyone liked and he seemed to have good synergies with everyone. As expected from his level of professional, he was highly knowledgeable of almost all facets of business and behaved more like a guide or mentor. He generally took a backseat after giving directions to his team and let them handle the execution part.*
>
> *Though Tom knew about the actual contribution of each team-member yet rarely expressed the same, in his behaviours. He was always more focused on utilizing skill-set of every team-member in the best possible manner without causing major dissonance in the team.*

While looking at inter-level synergies, at junior and middle levels, we may not be favourite of our managers because of our basic personality trait i.e. high thought process, knowledge and strategic bent of mind, which are expected from senior or top management professionals. This lack of synergy is because being Aristotle professionals, we are perceived as contributing little due to our not being involved in actual tasks on a daily basis and only talking or trying to talk things which people at senior levels should be doing. However, as Aristotle professionals, we are a big favourite or success when working in consultancy industry.

Hercules professionals or team-members remain top favourites of Aristotle personality type senior management professionals with Hypocrites and Parasite personality type juniors being our least favourites.

Professor Personality

At a junior level, if we display professor personality, we have average synergy (not high) synergy with most of the colleagues at same levels. This is so because our over-talkative behaviour takes some credibility off from the hard-work of others. Our colleagues feel as if we contribute less or equally but take extra credit because of better communication. We can observe that such professionals at middle levels display good synergies with all other personality types except colleagues with Free Rider and Parasite behaviours but the intensity of synergy or dissonance comes even closer to average, owing to suave or polished or even extra communication by them. At senior levels, if we display professor personality traits, we tend to have above average to good synergies with other Hercules, Aristotle, Professor and Passenger professionals. With the rest, we tend to display average to above average synergies because of their extrovert behaviour.

Looking at inter-level, we can observe that such professionals at a junior or middle management levels enjoy good synergies with higher levels in view of their ability to express or communicate more information within a short span of time, which they get for interactions with senior professionals. However, over-exposure to interactions with seniors might dent this synergy or positive perception. These professionals at senior levels are generally found to have good synergies with junior and middle management level professionals. These synergies are a result of their extrovert nature, free-flow of communication and they being perceived as more approachable by lower hierarchy level professionals.

Passenger Personality

Those of us who display passenger personality behaviours, irrespective of levels, we generally have good synergies with almost everyone in the team with hardly any dissonance. This is because we are rarely worried about what others are doing or not doing. We just do our work as a routine, to the best of our ability and aren't in competition with anyone. Our behaviour is the closest to being mindful behaviour in corporate settings and we are generally found to be at peace with ourselves and others.

Passenger personality professionals, at either level, have normal to good synergies with almost everyone at all levels. This results from the fact that everyone perceives them as harmless but contributing team-members, seniors or juniors. Even at senior management levels, they aren't considered a threat to team-spirit or to themselves by CEOs.

> *Major reason of synergy of passenger professionals with almost everyone at all levels is that the presence or absence of limelight, rewards or promotions doesn't impact their performance in a major way. They keep doing their job as usual. Their behaviour, personality and nature of considering a job as a job is their biggest asset.*

Hypocrite Personality

At a junior level, if our behaviours correspond to this personality type, we tend to display less synergies with almost all other professionals with intensity of dissonance being highest with Hercules, owing to extreme behaviours of

Hercules, followed by Aristotle professionals with higher intelligence. At middle levels, we show almost similar synergies or dissonances with lesser extremes owing to our ability to cover-up on things by extroversion and communication skills. Therefore we tend to start moving towards neutral synergies at middle levels except for our synergy with Hercules and Aristotle which continues being below average. At senior levels, our synergies generally improve from average to above average except for those with Hercules and Aristotle where it remains at below average and average levels respectively.

For inter-level synergies, at junior or middle levels, we are able to hide our dual speak due to our soft-skills and limited interactions with higher level professionals and therefore, enjoy good synergies. However, at middle or senior levels, we are not trusted by lower level employees. This dissonance isn't much visible until a lower level employee is asked to volunteer for a task under those of us who are a hypocrite seniors and we finds very few juniors raising their hands to volunteer for working in our teams. This happens because of the trust factor i.e. as managers, we aren't trusted by juniors.

Free rider Personality

Those of us who display this personality behaviours, at junior level, share poor synergies with our team-members because junior team-members work more closely, so can easily see the levels of contribution by others and employees at these levels are more forthcoming in expressing their likes or dislikes. At middle management levels, we tend to display below average synergies with Hercules, Aristotle and Mercenary colleagues owing to non-contribution and average synergies with the rest owing to ability to cover-up on things by communication skills or closeness to manager gained by extra flattery. At a senior level, except for Hercules and mercenary colleagues, we share average synergies.

At an inter-level, we don't enjoy good synergies with professionals at next levels, unless our manager hides our true personality by openly praising us. A manager might be doing so either to get rid of us or might have been gullible enough to fall for our flattery. If we reach senior levels, we are generally able to hide our personality from lower level employees owing to our nature and being visible at the right time and place. This may not continue for longer duration and eventually, lower level employees can see through the non-contributing nature of such seniors. Remember the adage of monkey climbing up the tree.

Mercenary Personality

Those of us who display mercenary personality behaviours, at junior levels, we are generally liked by our colleagues because of our zeal towards achieving team goals and very hard-working nature. Also, at these levels, our colleagues haven't yet developed the knowledge and importance of compliances and legal laws, which we are prone to neglecting from the very beginning. At middle levels, we tend to have above average or good synergies with our colleagues except the ones displaying parasitic behaviours. This happens because of our perception of ourselves being highly committed while knowing that parasitic managers neither contribute anything nor are committed. At senior levels, being mercenary professionals, we don't share good synergies with Hercules, free rider and parasite personality colleagues and share average synergies with the rest. A point to note here is that similar to Hercules, our Aristotle colleagues are also consciously aware of our personality traits but they are very mindful in their behaviours so on the surface, synergy seems to be average.

Looking at inter-level synergies, we, as Mercenary professionals at junior or middle management level, enjoy good synergies with our next levels because of our hard-work and soft-skills. And also because at this stage being or not being in conformity of compliances can't be visible much. So, we are perceived similar to Hercules professionals by our senior levels. Even at senior levels, we tend to enjoy good synergies with our lower levels except with Hercules and Aristotle personality type juniors. These two personality type junior level employees can see through the personalities of their mercenary type seniors and likely harmful impacts which might result due to the means taken or used by mercenary type senior level employees.

Parasite Personality

We can observe that professionals with parasite personality behaviours tend to have very low synergies with almost all their colleagues owing to their non-contribution as well as their perception of being harmful towards other colleagues. At middle level too, they will have dissonance with almost all their colleagues except other similar personality type colleagues because in this case such colleagues tend to become support systems of each other. Even at senior levels, their dissonance with colleagues continues but it is more pronounced in case of their interactions with Hercules and Aristotle colleagues.

We can observe that these professionals at lower levels of hierarchy might be able to camouflage their true nature from their seniors by resorting to being extra courteous and yes-men to their next level professionals during the limited interaction which they have with their next levels. So, they seem to enjoy good synergies unless it gets impacted by their manager's feedback. At a senior level too, such professionals are able to camouflage their true nature unless they become direct managers of those employees and then they realize the true nature of parasite personality type senior professionals, leading to major dissonance with certain specific personality type team-members.

As professionals, it is important for us to have good synergies across levels as it helps in creating a positive perception about us. Positive perception leads to better acceptance of us as team-members, colleagues or leaders and sense of acceptance always results in a feeling of happiness. This very positive perception and acceptance helps us grow in the organization or industry we are working in.

At the same time, the conscious awareness of dissonances and reasons thereof enables us to either transform ourselves to bring synergies or accept the dissonance. Accepting dissonance is similar to a situation where we agree to disagree on something and instead of taking that disagreement at a personal level, we keep it professional. Similarly, as a conscious aware professional we must accept the dissonances as part and parcel of human interactions and never stretch them to levels where these dissonances start impacting our peace of mind or career growth. Because in case either gets adversely affected, we will not be happy.

6. Black Swan

An important facet affecting our peace of mind and happiness in day-to-day work-life is our relationship with the team we are working with. This relationship and team-member's perceptions or our perceptions about the team have a major impact on our peace of mind, happiness and productivity because of the high frequency of interactions that we have with the immediate team that we are working with.

We must be consciously aware whether we feel and are also perceived to be a good team-member belonging to the same herd or we feel and are perceived to be a 'black swan' among team-members i.e. misfit, with others considering themselves to be white swans. A feeling of belongingness and acceptance as a team-members leads to happiness whereas a feeling of dissonance leads to inner turmoil.

Black Swan theory was developed by Nassim Nicholas Taleb. A black swan is an event or occurrence that deviates beyond what is normally expected of a situation and is extremely difficult to predict. Taleb has described his theory to explain financial events as he was a finance professor. A black swan event is a metaphor that describes an event that is a surprise to the observer, has a major effect and is often inappropriately rationalized retrospectively, with the benefit of hindsight.

In recent times in Indian business scenario, the rise of the Ayurveda based brand Patanjali was one such business event which was a surprise, had a major effect and every major competing brand i.e. Colgate, P&G etc. tried to rationalize it after it had happened because none of them had anticipated any such competition, on such a large scale.

Let us look at the black swan metaphor of Taleb, not from finance or business perspective but, from human dynamics perspective involving ourselves as professionals as well as our colleagues. In the below situation, Rajat joined a team, which had well-established culture of its own.

> *Rajat joined his new company which had an existing culture where the leader's decisions weren't normally questioned, even if someone considered the decision-making process or decision to be incorrect and not based on logic. Rajat happens to be one with independent thinking and logical in his approach and always ready to face questions and also question others. The existing team expected that Rajat will take some time and adjust to the existing culture. However, Rajat had his own personality and wasn't able to change much beyond a point. With passage of time, dissonance between Rajat and his team reached to extreme levels. For the existing team, he became a black swan and the situation threw new challenges for both, existing team and Rajat.*

Similar to the above case, it can also happen for an existing team and team-members and the 'black swan' professional need not be a new entrant in the team. This is because every organization is dynamic with professionals leaving and joining it regularly.

Before, we proceed further on what it means for a professional, manager or team to handle such stressful and difficult situations and what we should do about it; let us first see how we can assess whether we or someone else is a black swan or not or even a team or its leader can assess whether a particular team-member is a similar to black swan event.

Are we the black swan?

As professionals, sometimes we may feel suffocated working in an existing team and the feeling might have started affecting not only our professional output but our mental peace, family life and overall happiness at work and at home. This is the time when we need to take a break and some quite moments for ourselves. This time is not only for getting rejuvenated but also for some introspection and keen observation and analysis of the professional situations surrounding ourselves which drove us into these situations.

There is a very simple exercise we should indulge-in during this break. Objectively assess our existing relationships with our manager and colleagues, whether it is positive, negative or neutral. Once you have assessed all the relationships, depending on your team size, choose two or three close confidantes of your manager and count them as double i.e. each member as good as two. Ideally, your relationship with your manager must be positive. If it is positive, count it as two. However, if it is negative, count it as equivalent to three. Having done that, mark every positive as plus one and every negative as minus with neutral being equal to zero.

Now, we need to calculate the total score. A negative or zero score indicates that our synergies with our team are poor and we are a black swan. This doesn't imply that it is a negative ranking for us but it simply means that we aren't in sync with the team we are working with. This is a simple exercise for introspection and situation assessment.

If we feel we are a black swan i.e. we don't share a positive relationship with more than half of our team including our manager; then in spite of us being logically correct, highly ethical, highly professional, adding value to business and following highest standards of integrity, we may not be in synergy with your team. This may go against us professionally and personally.

We may also be perceived as a black swan if we have come from an organization whose culture is completely different from the culture of our present organization and we are still trying to follow what we learnt and followed in our previous culture i.e. we have come with a heavy baggage. Another case of us being considered a black swan can be when there are strong personality related differences between us and key members of our team who are not only opinion-makers but also close to our manager and who have strong impact on our manager's behaviour, impacting our relationship with our manager.

Having analysed the situation, the endeavour should be to reach the ideal situation i.e. we must be having positive relationships with maximum of our team-members and the rest should fall in neutral category instead of negative. However, it may not always be advisable to waste lot of energies on moving away from 'black swan' situation. For example – whether it is our manager, team or organization; if we reach a conclusion that we are a complete misfit in the team as well as organizational culture, then spending energies on finding a suitable job and switching job is better idea than staying and trying to change. It gives better results in career progression and peace in personal life.

Bringing Synergies with Our Team

We can't keep switching the jobs and it may not always be possible. Therefore, in such situations, displaying mindful behaviours can always improve the situation. If we don't share a positive relationship with our manager, then that is the first area to work upon. This has been discussed in detail in subsequent chapters titled 'We and Our Manager' and 'Are we valued".

Next focus area to quickly and consciously turn-around the situation towards bringing positivity and moving away from 'black swan' situation is focusing on our relationships with close confidants of our manager. This doesn't mean that we must be great friends with them but focus on improving our working relationships and avoiding areas of confrontation at all times. These are the colleagues who can prove to be most dangerous for us because they can spoil our positive relationship with our manager, in due course of time, through constant negative feedback. This is even easier for them if you are located away from your manager's location.

Then, we must look for Professor Personality team-members and improve our synergies with them because these are the team-members who are opinion-makers and speak a lot in the team. If these team-members are speaking positive about us, then they can be effective brand managers for us. Seeking help from senior team-members on finding-out the areas which needs to be worked upon by us to become a better team-member also helps bringing more synergies.

It always helps to try and take-out extremes from our behaviour as far as possible. A lot of times, our social behaviour ruins our hard-work. For example, a team-member who is very hard-working but also indulges in gossiping isn't a preferred team-member. So in work-settings it is always advisable to be professional.

As a manager or leader, we have a bigger responsibility if we find an employee to be in such a 'black swan' situation. We should neither believe that helping such team-members is waste of time and energy nor think that other team-members may get affected if we pays extra attention to such a team-member. As leaders, we must always try and improve the situation by having a detailed discussion with the employee to understand the concerns and providing reasoning of why you (as leader and rest of the team) are doing what you are doing. Asking for view-point, areas of concern and providing a patient listening helps such a team-member getting into the team spirit. We must take suggestions or ideas of such team-members and consider them as 'out of box' ideas to understand them better. Additionally, it helps to provide a mentor to such team-members.

As a leader, if we observe that a particular team-member is in a black swan situation because of serious differences with some team-members then using conflict-resolution strategies such as formal meetings between such employees, giving same tasks to such conflicting members so that they have to work together as a team to be successful and improving communication among such team members. It is always beneficial to work positively and resolve the situation because teams always perform better in positive work-setting.

We need to be consciously aware of our synergies with colleagues as impact of these synergies goes beyond performance. However, organizations comprise of various hierarchical levels and therefore, it is also important for us to assess and be consciously aware of the synergy between employees at inter-hierarchical levels i.e. between junior and middle-management or between middle and senior management.

8. Interacting With or As Manager

"An employee's motivation is a direct result of the sum of interaction with his/her manager." Dr. Bob Nelson

Millions of professionals leave their jobs every month and while they are doing so, many more millions are spending a lot of time and energy on finding a new job, so that they can leave their existing job. Effectively, all these people are not happy with their jobs to an extent where they are willing to go through the painful change management process of changing work-place, colleagues, organization and may be residence location, kid's school and consequent turmoil for themselves and their families.

If each one of them was asked to honestly state the reason for quitting or wanting to quit, more than half would say 'they are leaving or want to leave because of their boss or manager'. Such is the effect or importance of a manager or boss in life of professionals. At the same time, we all have been, are and will be on either side of the table.

However, we can't choose or change our manager and we have to work with whosoever we get as our manager. If we are someone who is blessed with being managed by a manager, who has all the qualities that we expected from him, we are one of the luckiest professionals. As professionals, we take our manager's strengths for granted as every employee expects one's manager to be the ideal one, possessing all leadership qualities. The focus often remains on our manager's faults or weaknesses. A famous tribal adage explains the situation more aptly – *"as a monkey rises up the tree, its bottom is the only thing that is visible to other monkeys on the ground."*

If we open internet, we find innumerable number of articles advising on ways to manage our boss or manager. Though majority of those suggestions are really good but can they be applied universally? Applying them universally will be similar to a doctor providing a single prescription to all its patients for each and every kind of illness. So, for all those excellent ideas and articles to be more effective, we need to understand the underlying factors affecting the human dynamics between us and our manager because we both have unique personalities of our.

Our interaction with manager has four very important factors i.e. our personality, our manager's personality, company's culture and organization type. Unless these factors and their interactions are looked at in greater detail, there is no use trying to fix the problem. Isn't a proper diagnosis needed before any prescription? In this section we shall look at the possibility, or not, of synergy between our personality and our manager's personality. If there are possibilities of synergy, what can be done to improve that synergy? If there is no synergy, what can be done to reduce the dissonance, which we might be already feeling and when it is time to move-out from the team of our current manager?

Personality attributes

In the section on synergies or dissonances between personalities across hierarchical levels in work-settings, we discussed this topic but since our relationship with our manager is one of the most important relationships affecting our job, career, mental peace and happiness, let us delve a bit deeper into the synergy or dissonance between us and our manager and which factors impact this synergy.

At different managerial levels, requirements of job are different and therefore managerial expectations from their team also change accordingly. However, interaction of personalities between us and our manager will always be highly affected by personality attributes of either, apart from the work culture. A major factor while looking at this interaction is the heavy bias towards what a manager considers to be synergy or what he likes or dislikes. This bias happens due to hierarchical advantage which every manager enjoys in the work-setting. Yet, how we, as professionals feels about our manager too has an effect on the synergy because synergy is two-way process. But we will focus on what we, as managers, expect from our team-members and how our personality affects our synergies with team-members.

As managers, we expect a lot from our team-members in terms of skills, behaviour, team-working, taking extra initiative or covering-up their manager's i.e. our faults or delivering on targets irrespective of compliances etc. depending on our personality type. Though, the analysis and discussion focuses on the expectations on either side i.e. us as team-members and us as manager from the perspective of various personality types, yet owing to the higher impact of manager's expectations as well as personality, the focus will be certainly biased with more weightage being given to our personality as a manager and our liking and disliking for various personality type team-members impacting synergies or dissonances. Even as team-members, we always need to consciously aware of what our manager expects from us or what we, as manager, expect from our teams based on our personality traits.

Hercules Manager

If we, as manager, display Herculean Personality, then we will have strong opinions and likes or dislikes among our team members. We can generally see through people's personalities and we prefer people who actually help in delivering on the assigned tasks or targets in a compliant manner. Owing to this reason, we tend to display extreme liking for herculean team-members and strong dislikes for personality types displaying free-rider, hypocrite and parasite traits. Accordingly, there will be possibility of high synergies of a herculean manager with a herculean employee whereas strong dissonance with the free-rider, hypocrite and parasite personality type team-members.

Those employees who display professor, passenger or mercenary traits will generally have average to above average synergy with us as a herculean manager. These personality type employees may not be in our best books but we understand skill-sets of these employees and know that with our guidance, they will be able to contribute.

To improve synergies with us i.e. a herculean manager, a team-member with professor type personality must talks less, passenger must work slightly harder and take initiative sometimes whereas a mercenary type personality needs to become very conscious of compliances. There is very less possibility of any synergies between team-members displaying either free-Rider or Hypocrite or Parasite personality types and us, as herculean managers unless those team-members start contributing as per their hierarchical level and assigned roles. Such team-members either need to change their personalities completely or move-out of our i.e. a herculean manager's team as soon as possible.

The above is true when we ourselves, as Hercules managers, are at middle or senior management level. But what is the probability of our synergy or dissonance as a senior management professional ourselves with our CEO or MD?

Mike was a senior professional who faced severe dissonance with John, his MD, because of factors such as over-enthusiasm displayed by Mike about organizational goals and not being conscious of views of John. Mike was regarded highly among his team-members but consciously or unconsciously used to display emotions and was emotional towards his teams as well as organization. John expected Mike to be bereft of emotions in the name of emotional quotient required for senior professionals.

Mike was highly ethical and idealistic and expected the same from others especially from John. When John fell short of his expectations, dissonance between the two started becoming visible. Similarly, due to Mike's goal-orientation and over-achievement of business goals, John perceived him as a threat to his own position and therefore started downplaying Mike's achievements. This led to major dissonance between Mike and his MD, John who just wanted to keep his position secure, didn't have high ethical standards and always took credit for success and blamed his teams for failures.

However, ultimately this dissonance didn't prove right for Mike's career and overall happiness for himself and his team. We all need to be consciously aware of our dissonances and avoid taking extreme positions. After all, it is just a job and not our entire life.

Similar to the case of Mike who was a Hercules senior professional, it is important for us to not only be consciously aware of our personality type but also personality type of our manager and the existing dissonance with our CEOs and also the reasons thereof. Reducing this dissonance and achieving synergy is possible only once we becomes consciously aware of the dissonance and reasons of the dissonance.

Aristotle Manager

If we as managers display Aristotle Personality traits, then we will be more thoughtful and slightly less action-oriented. We prefer taking backseat after providing a direction or strategy and let our team do the needful. We tend not to display extreme likes and dislikes as a Hercules manager would do.

We always need herculean team-members to implement our thoughts and since a herculean employee is more action-oriented so we complement each-other and therefore probability of synergy is high. The only chance of dissonance between Aristotle manager and herculean team-member will be when we, as a manager portray or pretends to be of Aristotle personality but actually don't have Aristotle personality. In such a case, we will start feeling threatened and over-taken in the hierarchy by the action-oriented personality of our team-member. These are common incidents at senior hierarchical levels in organizations and also major reason of personality clashes and sometimes de-motivation in the entire team. Mike's case was a similar one wherein his MD pretended to be Aristotle but actually wasn't an Aristotle manager.

Team-members with Aristotle, Passenger or Professor Personality types will have above average synergies with us as Aristotle managers. This is because we are wise enough to see that these people bring value on the table in one or the other way. For example, we utilize extrovert nature of a professor team-member in customer-facing roles or as a trouble-shooter in the team. However, other personality types have below average synergies with us due to the fact that, though we may not be actually involved in action yet we can see through people's double speak or non-contribution because of our higher mental capabilities or thoughtfulness. We may not openly display this dislike or lack of synergies but the same can be observed during allocation of tasks or annual appraisals.

Professor Manager

We, as Professor Personality managers, might be highly talkative and full of I, Me, Myself attitude with lots of stories telling to the team and our team-meetings ending-up as another session of one-way talking by us, with little or no outcome of the meeting. This doesn't mean, we don't have knowledge but it only means we are highly talkative and if we become polished and suave in our talking, a lot of times our talks can be perceived highly impressive by first or second time listeners.

Being such managers, we don't have extreme likes and dislikes and whoever can patiently listen to us will have good synergies with us. We want someone to execute the work and therefore will have better synergies with mercenary personality type employees, as such employees don't question us i.e. their manager and just execute the directions irrespective of compliances. For the Team-members, it is slightly easy to bring or improve synergies with us and for that they only need to be good listeners and never questioning their managers.

In one's corporate life, one finds managers like us at all hierarchical levels of the organization but more so at middle or senior management levels because we would have been individual contributors (sales, commercial or customer service kind of roles) or managing remote teams before reaching senior levels.

Passenger Manager

We, as Passenger Personality managers, take-up every managerial role with a view to remain in the role for a pre-decided time i.e. generally 2-3 years. Being such managers, we want to just bid time, complete targets, not get into unnecessary big things and resultant controversies and then move-on to some next role in the same company or a different company. We generally best fit in subsidiaries of multinational companies where everyone has a defined role and which runs on processes instead of managerial capability.

Team-members with Herculean Personality will have good synergies with us in the beginning but such employees start getting confused with time while working with us. The major reason for this confusion or dissonance is that we, as managers, don't distinguish much between our employees and treat performers and non-performers almost equally. This leads to a Herculean team-member thinking and feeling uselessness of putting extra efforts and this also starts getting visible in his/her behaviour patterns.

Team-members with Mercenary Personality traits have good synergies with us as we want the tasks or targets to be met and even if there are legal or compliances being overlooked. We are aware that such things will take time to come to notice of our higher-up or legal authorities and even if that happens, it is easier to feign ignorance and put the blame on team-members. However, we don't go over-board in letting non-compliances happen.

We are consciously aware of our being passengers for some time in the journey, therefore we maintain cordial relations and synergy with every team-member and avoid dissonance. Though we might pretend to have concern for every team-member's career as well as organization but in reality, we are always counting the time left before we jump the ship and if possible, gain a bigger role or salary in the process.

Before we move forward discussing the synergy scale of an employee with managers displaying personality traits of Hypocrite, Free Rider, Mercenary or Parasite type, we need to be conscious of the fact that such managers are the ones who aren't leaders in true sense but just managers who happen to be where they are because of reasons other than leadership skills.

Hypocrite Manager

We can observe that a Manager who displays Hypocrite Personality traits is someone who follows double standards i.e. one set of values, morals or ethics for themselves and in situations which might affect them and another set of values, morals or ethics for others or situations involving team-members. Such managers are generally suave and very good actors and they easily earn sympathies of their team-members by presenting a *bechara* (i.e. simple, helpless, poor, harmless guy) image of themselves.

It is easy for us to observe that such managers have good synergies with Mercenary and Passenger team-members because ultimately such managers prefer team-members who deliver on the results without asking questions or looking through manager's hypocrite nature. However, such managers have very low possibility of synergies with team-members having Herculean personalities because of two reasons; one, herculean team-members always looks for managers with straight-forward, ethical behaviours and don't prefer hypocrite people and second, a hypocrite manager feels threatened by the energy, regard and respect of herculean team-member among his/her colleagues or teams.

Team-members with Aristotle, Hypocrite, Free Rider and Parasite Personality traits will have average or above average working synergies with such a manager. However, such managers are generally aware of true nature of their team-members and therefore even though these managers may pretend to have average synergies through-out the year, yet harm the employees during annual appraisals. Similarly, if ego of such managers is hurt, they can keep it hidden, for long periods of time, till they are in a situation when they can take their revenge. While in the process of seeking revenge, hypocrite managers can go to any extent such as sabotaging careers and even terminating such team-members from the jobs through well-planned conspiracy, in such a way that the manager still seems to be simple and innocent to the rest.

As professionals, we need to be very careful while working with managers with hypocrite personality traits and it is always advisable to tread a middle path and try to display behaviour traits of a passenger personality type. If we are aware that we have herculean personality behaviour traits, we must move out from the team of such a manager as soon as possible.

Free Rider Manager

We can observe that a Manager who displays Free Rider Personality traits is someone who brings nothing to the table except his/her hierarchical position and wants the team to do everything. Such managers will tend to appropriate all the credit for success but will never own responsibility for failure.

Such managers will have high probability of synergy with team-members displaying Herculean, Aristotle, Professor,

Passenger and Mercenary Personality types because such team-members bring value in their own way and a manager with free rider personality would always prefer people who work, so that he/she doesn't have to work. However, team-members with hypocrite, free rider and parasite personality type will have low probability of synergy with such managers owing to the fact that free rider personality managers know the fact that they themselves aren't contributing much and therefore don't need team-members who also don't bring anything on the table.

Mercenary Manager

We can observe that a Manager who displays Mercenary Personality traits tends to have very high energy levels, is demagogic in communication, gives results overlooking ethics or legal compliances and pretends to follow a higher set of values. Such manager wants to reach goals at any cost.

Team-members with similar personality traits i.e. mercenary will have very high synergy with such managers. Since a herculean team-member is full of energy, he/she will have high synergy with a mercenary manager till there is a clash of point-of-view regarding ethics, morals and values. Whereas an Aristotle team-member, owing to higher thought-process and ability to see through a mercenary, will have average synergy but will deftly avoid being part of unethical ways and means of such managers.

Team-members with professor and passenger personalities will generally have good synergies with a mercenary manager. Because neither they are part of inner coterie of such managers nor they are much concerned with their aims and motives. Since a team-member with professor personality speaks a lot and create perceptions, so such managers might want to keep them in good books and also use them to create positive perceptions for themselves wherever they can. Team-members with hypocrite, free rider and parasite personality type don't have good synergies with such managers and there is always dissonance or mercenary managers neglect such employees.

From professional's point-of-view, if we have realized that our manager is a mercenary and if the organization is valuing him / her highly; then in extreme circumstances, an Enron type situation might be the final result and we need to be very careful. If we aren't a mercenary ourselves, then working for such managers can ruin our career or even life due to non-compliance of legal laws.

Parasite Manager

We can observe that a Manager who displays Parasite Personality traits is someone who tends to have personality which is a combination of free rider and hypocrite and therefore there will be good synergy between such manager and team members with mercenary, passenger and professor personality traits.

There will be lot of dissonance between such managers and team-members with parasite, free rider and hypocrite personality type and average synergy with herculean and Aristotle personality team-members. Such managers never take responsibilities and openly criticize their team members for smallest of the mistakes. They take all the credit for the work and blame their team-members for everything that didn't work-out.

Can synergy be improved or dissonance be reduced?

Improving synergies where the dissonances aren't extreme is much easier. For that we need to look at the dissonance areas and try being slightly more mindful in our behaviours. However, we also need to remember that bringing complete synergies is never possible because two personalities will always have some dissonance and that is healthy for both.

For specific personality types, there are two stages of dissonance between them and their managers. First stage is where dissonance is at a neutral level i.e. areas of synergy or dissonance are almost equal; and second, where dissonances are high so probability of synergy is very slim. In the first case, dissonance can be reduced by us as a team-member, to a working level i.e. taken to a level where areas of synergy are more than dissonance, by managing our behaviours and being more mindful. However, in the second case, even if we wants to bring-in synergy, it will be short-lived and we may need to completely change our personality, which is humanly not possible.

However, our first try and that of every corporate professional ought to be reducing dissonance and improving synergies with our manager and for this we must take conscious steps.

How to reduce dissonance and improve synergies?

The first step in improving our synergies with our manager is being consciously aware about the importance of our relationship and synergy with our manager in the work-place and the effect it has on our other relationships with colleagues, seniors as well as on career growth. This conscious awareness helps us in knowing becoming aware as to why we need to put extra efforts in our endeavour to improve synergies with our manager.

Our manager has a role to play in the organization and even if we perceive him to be incompetent or not a good manager / leader, we must at least give him this much due that he has reached where he has, because he must be having some qualities, skills or something unique about him. We need to find-out those functional and behavioural skills in our manager which might have helped him reach where he has. We should objectively observe him to access him i.e. personality traits, strengths and weaknesses and never try to speak about or highlight, in our behaviour, his/her weaknesses in person or public.

It helps if we list-out the areas of synergy or dissonance and then reinforce areas of synergy and find-out what our manager expects from us regarding the areas of dissonance. We should try to be more mindful in those areas and manage our behaviour. Finding-out our manager's expectations from us on the deliverables and if possible, having it documented always helps us, though it will depend on the type of organization, its culture and also personality type of our manager. We shouldn't be rigid about getting it documented but at least we must try to do that. Also, it helps to bring synergies if we seek feedback on our behavioural aspects and be open to manage our behaviour where our manager expects us to be more mindful.

We must take conscious actions or steps for improving synergies with our manager for our peace of mind, happiness and career growth. However, if our personality traits and those of our manager don't match at all i.e. very low probability of synergy, it might be quite utopian to talk about bringing synergies, as much as we may try. We may read any number of books or seek guidance from mentors or coaches or be highly mindful yet the dissonances will come to the surface at unexpected moments. If our efforts to bring synergies fail and if we had put-in these efforts despite being consciously aware of no possibility of bringing synergies, then we may feel even more dejected and unhappy as to what was the need to waste so much of time trying to alter behaviours. The inner conflicts in the mind will also weigh heavily at all times while trying to bring synergies among completely different personalities.

In addition to analysing and trying to improve our synergy with our manager, using the above discussed synergy scale between various personality types, there are some tale-tell signs in the behaviour of our manager, which can always let us know if our manager values us.

Also, as managers we must be consciously aware of our behaviours because we might be unconsciously sending wrong signals to our team-members. These behaviours will not only bring dissonance, demoralization and unhappiness for the team-members but also are major factors in our professional failures and resulting unhappiness. It might in a feeling and afterthought as to what went wrong. Our not being consciously aware of our behaviour, as a manager, is what went wrong and which resulted in differences, demoralizing of team-members and everyone being in a lose-lose situation. Therefore, we, as managers, must be consciously aware of effects of our behaviour and its impact on happiness in the entire team.

9. Are We Valued?

"These days man knows price of everything but the 'value' of nothing." – Oscar Wilde

We always keep wondering and grappling with a constant question or dilemma – "Does my manager value me?" This thought, question or dilemma affects our inner peace and happiness in a major way because a feeling of being valued results in contentment, satisfaction and happiness.

We are never alone and everyone goes through this dilemma sometime or other in their work life. However, sometimes it might be just a misunderstanding on our part or in other cases, it might be true also. Therefore, an objective analysis of the problem in hand will enable us to know and be consciously aware whether we are valued or not. It will help us in focusing our energies in a more positive direction, if it is just a misunderstanding. In case, even after an objective analysis, we reach a conclusion that our manager doesn't value us, then this analysis will help us in making some important decisions.

But before we move forward discussing this important topic, let us see what the word 'value' means. The Oxford Dictionary, while referring to the word 'value' as a noun, defines it as "the regard that something is held to deserve; the importance, worth or usefulness of something" and while referring to word 'value' as a verb, it is one which is "considered (someone or something) to be important or beneficial; have a high opinion of".

While referring to these definitions in the context of us, as professionals in work-life, a few words from the above definitions which become important are: regard, deserve, usefulness, importance, worth, considered and high opinion. So, we might need to focus on some important areas such as, Are we getting the regard or respect, from our manager, that every professional deserves as a human being; are we considered to be useful, beneficial and important by our manager; is our real worth being paid which in work-life means are we getting paid commensurate to our contribution; and does our manager hold us in high opinion or not?

There are very rare cases wherein managers might be willing to answer these questions directly and even asking these questions directly or subtly from our manager might jeopardize our career progression. However, there may be some subtle gestures or messages that manager might be sending to us and maybe we need to be observant about our manager's behaviours for some time and then analyse the same.

Visibility

The word 'visibility' is generally used in weather conditions and it means 'how far or how clearly one can see in particular weather conditions'. If the word is used to refer to visibility of something i.e. situation, problem or individual, it means 'how much it is seen or noticed by other people'.In work-life parlance, our visibility refers to how much we are seen or noticed by other people specially higher-ups. A manager can always positively or negatively affect the degree of visibility that we get in the organization through various actions such as, inviting or not inviting us to crucial meetings involving important customers or senior management, visits by senior-management leadership, restricted-entry social events such as top-management formal dinners etc.

We must be observant enough to find-out whether we are visible as a critical team member when there are senior management visits from Head Quarters or corporate offices or are we being invited for high profile customer meetings or are we also part of senior management social events, when some of our colleagues are part of it.

If we observe that the above observations provide a positive response, then it implies our manager values us and a negative response means the opposite and implies that we aren't valued by our manager and our secondary status is clear.

Our Participation blocked

A manager is supposed to provide equal opportunity to all his team-members to participate in important discussions related to high-profile projects and strategy and utilize their skills and experience. Now, in case our manager isn't inviting us to such important discussions even when the discussions are about our sphere of influence, then it is a matter of concern.

In case, we are that professional who is not only not being invited but also our entry is being blocked on one or another pretext, this implies that we are not on our manager's priority list and he considers us to be a just another passenger on the train. Sometimes, not only we aren't invited for participating in important discussions but our manager might be giving us insignificant tasks so that we won't be able to focus on our real job and we will miss our goals.

In fact, these gestures imply that our manager doesn't value our knowledge, skills or experience but wants us to keep doing the mundane tasks that we are doing so that we get bored and quit or else our career progression is halted.

Communication Patterns

In an organization, three primary communication channels are face-to-face verbal communication, phone calls and emails. Depending on the physical distance between us and our manager, frequency of using these channels vary. An ideal situation is regular timely communication with either side reciprocating to the other side. However, a few communication related behaviour patterns need to be observed carefully.

> *Sam started noticing certain communication behaviours in his new manager, Singh. He noticed that Singh hasn't been replying to his mails / messages quick enough or as good as he did so for others. Most of the times, he didn't take Sam's call and sent a message saying I am busy or can we talk later, which, unfortunately, rarely happened. Similarly, whenever he sought meeting time from Singh, he didn't spare time for meeting Sam as quickly or as much as he did for other team-members. Most odd thing to notice was that Singh had started communicating with Sam mostly via emails and had been copying HR lady in the mails.*

If we find such behaviour patterns or gestures from our manager, then our manager may be sending a subtle signal to us that we aren't valued as his/her team-member.

Accessibility to our manager

What does it mean to be accessible? Accessible, while referring to a person in authority, means approachable and friendly or easy to talk to. Similarly, in a corporate situation, our manager is considered accessible to us if he/she listens intently to our problems, suggestions or ideas and gives solutions or feedback as he/she deems fit.

Sonal seemed a bit worried. She confided in her friend Ram. Sonal – "My manager isn't accessible and approachable at all. He rarely smiles and isn't easy to talk to. He wants to hear only good news and overreacts to bad news. He doesn't listen to and consider suggestions which contradict his own thought-process. He enjoys the fact that employees keep quite when he walks by? What should I do?" Ram told her – "If your manager is neither accessible / approachable to you nor to the entire team, then it is his personality issue. However, if he is readily accessible to your colleagues but not to you, then your manager's priorities lie somewhere else and he/she doesn't value you."

Friendly Bantering, Gossip or Rumours

A lot of communication in organizations can be described as friendly bantering and gossips / rumours, which primarily involves speaking at the back of a colleague, manager or team-member. We must always be part of friendly bantering but shouldn't involve in ourselves in gossips, though we must very keenly observes which way gossips are going. A few times, we might observe that our manager often do friendly teasing with other team-members of your team but never feels comfortable including you in friendly bantering. Sometimes, we observe that our manager talks about us with our colleagues, specially pointing-out our flaws, and they tell us about the same, particularly those colleagues who are seen as close to manager or else, our manager talks negatively about us in front of other managers or other higher-ups.

Sometimes, our manager not only keeps quite but also enjoys when our colleagues are ridiculing or mocking us or speaking derogatively about us in our presence or absence.

Due appreciation

Does our boss appreciate us in public and gives due recognition for our achievements or we have been noticing opposite behaviours being displayed by our manager.

> *Ravi's team achieved highest engagement score globally and he told his manager i.e. CEO. The first sign he saw on face of CEO was irritation & frustration and not satisfaction and pride. Even when CEOs colleagues praised Ravi, the emotion on the face of his manager used to be jealousy or even rage indicating – how dare you take the spotlight off me. He even picked on Ravi for smallest of issues, highlighting his weaknesses publicly and letting him down in public.*

If we notice similar behavioural patterns from our manager, then it implies that he hardly cares for us or he wants us to be demotivated enough so that we can choose our way.

Feedback

Good managers provide precise, timely and constructive feedback. Does our manager provide the same or not? We may observe that our manager gives no feedback to us about anything that you do. So, we have no idea whether we are doing things right or wrong or if any course-correction is needed. If we ask our manager for a feedback, we get a generalized answer – 'Oh, you are doing fine' or 'keep doing what you are doing'. Even if our manager decides to give us feedback, he gives positive feedback privately and negative feedback publicly.

If the above behaviour patterns are common for us as well as our colleagues, then it is an issue with our manager's leadership skills. However, if the above behaviour patterns are only meant for us, then it is a serious concern and we must realize that he doesn't value our contribution.

Career guidance

In an ideal situation and organizational culture, a manager has the responsibility to provide career guidance to team-members and see that they grow in their careers. We are responsible for our career progression but to ensure the same, our manager's support is very crucial. Therefore, we must proactively observe and find answers to questions such as - Does our manager ever have had discussions regarding our career goals and if yes, does he subsequently follow-up on the agreed areas to make sure our career progresses?

If the answer to above questions is - no, then our manager hardly cares for us and our career progression. He is only concerned as to how much he can squeeze us to further his goals.

Appraisal discussion and Pay-out

Performance appraisals provide the opportunity to recognize and reward employees and to ensure they feel valued for the work that they do. The biggest sign of our value, as professionals in a manager's team, will be visible during our appraisal discussion and pay-out. So, we need to be very observant about some key behaviour patterns.

Whether or not our manager does face-to-face, objective and two-way appraisal discussion spending sufficient time. Did we come-out of the appraisal discussion with rejuvenated energy and clarity on the way-forward for us? Did he spend sufficient time praising us for our good work and explaining our improvement areas and how he/she is going to help us improve ourselves? Is our pay-out commensurate to our hard-work?

If we find a positive answer to the above questions, then we are a valued team-member and if we find the answer to be no for most of these, then we may not be a valuable team member for our manager.

*

Once we have observed the above parameters very objectively, we might find that, in case of most of the above discussed points, our manager values us and that most of our fears weren't fact-based. However, we may also come to a conclusion that we found most of the answers to be 'no' and that our manager doesn't value us.

In the later scenario, we have a dilemma in front of us and instead of getting bogged down and de-motivated, we need to start working proactively on several fronts. We must always remember that in corporate world, when a situation comes between choosing either an employee or manager, manager gets priority, so there is no use fighting with our manager and taking the situation to extremes. However, we can certainly take some proactive steps to improve the situation. Two cases of Ritesh and Aseem help us understand the dilemma and resulting pro-active actions taken by them.

Ritesh scheduled a meeting with Sia, his manager and politely discussed his worries with her. Sia appreciated initiative taken by Ritesh and spelled-out the steps that he needed to take-up to become a valued member of her team. He worked on the areas suggested by Sia and was pleasantly surprized to find himself in the promotion list next year.

Aseem was feeling that his manager Danny didn't value him and he wasn't even willing to discuss the same with Aseem. Finally, Aseem brought his dilemma to the notice two members of the senior management leadership, who were more sympathetic towards him and knew his real worth. Aseem got a new assignment with one of the senior management leaders and continued his corporate journey with career progressions and self-satisfaction.

We must take a deeper look at the personality types of both, us and our manager, to access if the differences are due to basic personality differences. If there are serious personality differences, then it may be difficult to bridge the gap. However, if there are minor differences, it is advisable to be mindful and work towards working collaboratively till we find a new job.

In corporate life, similar to social or political life, our connections at cross-functional and across leadership levels are always very helpful. If we have been able to build such relationships, we must proactively seek roles under a manager who is more likely to value us.

In case, even after taking first four steps outlined above, we still find ourselves stuck at the same place and in similar situation, there is no use wasting our time in trying to prove that we deserve better treatment and support from our manager. We must reconcile to the fact that, we are not lucky enough to be working with a manager with his/her specific personality and insecurities.

In such a scenario, we should be ideally focusing our energies on getting a new assignment. As professionals, we must always keep our channels with recruiters open. While we might or might not be taking above stated actions, it is advisable to tell the recruiters that we want to switch organization as early as possible. Our peace of mind, and happiness should take priority over proving who is right. As a consciously aware professional, it helps if we focus our energies and efforts towards our peace of mind, career progression and happiness.

*

'Our value doesn't decrease based on someone's inability to see our worth.'

As a consciously aware professional, we must always endeavour to value ourselves before expecting others to value us. Neither appreciation should take us to dizzying heights nor should criticism nor being not valued result in feeling unwanted and depressed. Our Conscious awareness helps us reach this balance. This conscious awareness and balance provides us with a feeling of happiness in either situation because we are aware that appreciation or being valued or career progression has lot of factors which aren't in our control but what we can certainly control is how we perceive them through conscious awareness. This enables us not letting these external factors control our happiness or decide happiness for us.

10. Organizational Culture

"Culture is more often a source of conflict than of synergy.
Cultural differences are a nuisance at best and often a disaster."
– Geert Hofstede

The workplace environment is a major factor affecting happiness of each of us and mostly we find that this very environment is making us unhappy. What determines workplace environment? Apart from human stakeholders i.e. ourselves, our colleagues and managers, it the organizational culture which generally determines the workplace environment. Knowing and understanding what is organizational culture and being consciously aware of our organization's culture enables us assess whether our personality and moral and ethical values are in sync with our organization.

The word 'culture' derives from a French term, which in turn derives from Latin *'colere'*, which means to tend to the earth and grow, or cultivation and nurture. Cambridge Dictionary defines culture as 'the way of life, especially the general customs and beliefs, of a particular group of people at a particular time'. Merriam-Webster announced 'culture' as their 2014 'Word of the year'. Their editors explained that they announced it their word of the year because the word 'culture' saw the biggest spike in look-up on their web site and that the confusion about word culture was the culture that year.

Organizational Culture

Organizational culture is a system of shared assumptions, values and beliefs, which govern how people behave in organizations. These shared values have a strong influence on the people in the organization and dictate how they dress, act and perform their jobs.

We can delve very deep in defining and exploring organizational culture by using definitions and types used by Edgar Schein, Robert A Cooke, Hofstede or Charles Handy but that would take us towards literary, psychological or sociological realm and away from our core purpose i.e. how we, as professionals, as a laymen busy with our taxing work routine, look at our organization and what parameters are important to us while looking at culture prevalent in our organization based on those parameters, at a given point of time.

Every organization is dynamic entity with no fixed population and lot of inward and outward movement of people, processes, factors affecting them etc. happening at any point of time. In view of the same, culture in any organization is also quite dynamic with no fixed set of beliefs, ideas or behaviour patterns and even if beliefs or ideas seem fixed, there is a constant churning going on either due to change in leadership or business environment or laws of the land.

Apart from other factors, organizational structure, ageing of an organization and local culture where the organization (or part of it) exist have a very deep impact on its culture. Company Structure has an impact on its culture, at a particular point of time, because structure determines the areas of influence (profit, processes, values, ethics, corporate governance etc.) and power-centres (owner, several owners, shareholders, senior management, a single leader etc.) in an organization.

In organizations, culture can also be an aspirational word i.e. a company might define or brand itself as one having "culture of accountability" or "culture of transparency" or "Performance-driven culture" but in actual sense, it may not have either of them. Similarly, there may be two or more parts i.e. subsidiaries of a company separated by national boundaries, state boundaries, cities, different parts of the same city or sometimes on different floors in the same high-rise building and in spite of them being from the same company or organization, the prevalent cultures may be entirely different.

Parameters

There are various parameters on which we define or give particular names, acronyms or nomenclature to organizational cultures prevalent at a given point of time at a given location in a company. These parameters can be respect or fairness, trust or integrity, change acceptance or adaptability, result orientation, teamwork, responsibility or accountability, employee welfare or learning and growth opportunities, meaning or purpose, communication styles, decision-making, goals or strategy, values or ethics, corporate governance etc.

While looking at various parameters from our i.e. professional's perspective when we observes our organizational culture, we find some significant parameters such as what is important for the organization (profits, customer, employees, society or the eco-system), how the organization does its business (importance of values, ethics, corporate governance and processes), interpersonal behaviours (justice, fairness, trust, integrity, accountability) and communication styles (transparent, purpose or meaning explained, secrecy around decision-making).

Though each of these parameters can be looked at and taken into consideration but what is important from our point of view and what our priority among the various parameters is needs to be consciously ascertained and depends on our personality and values. For example, for some of us, important parameters may be respect and fairness, growth opportunities and responsibility or accountability taking precedence over other parameters; whereas, for others, important parameters may be adaptability, teamwork and communication style.

Organizational Culture Types

While looking at various organizations from the above mentioned broad parameters and the importance given to one or more of these parameters, we can broadly divide the prevalent organizational cultures emphasizing or not emphasizing some cultural patterns.

Profit-Oriented Culture

In a profit-oriented company culture, the owners or top-management of a company gives utmost importance and top-priority to only its profits. Since profits depend on the customers, they too get their due importance. However, employees, their welfare, training or growth is secondary.

An organization or company having a purely profit-oriented culture will not give any importance to values, ethics or corporate governance and whenever they can make money by bypassing legal laws, they will do so. When it comes to interpersonal behaviours, such organizations have strict accountability, but only for financial targets and management or leadership can't be trusted as far as fairness, justice, trust or integrity are concerned.

Communication in such organizations is one-way i.e. from top-to-bottom of the hierarchy and there is complete secrecy around decision-making and purpose or meaning of strategy or decisions is never shared. Employees or departments generally work in silos in such companies.

Ethics - Oriented Culture

Cambridge Dictionary defines 'ethical' as 'relating to beliefs about what is morally right and wrong. Business Dictionary defines 'ethical' as equitable, fair and just dealing with people that, although pragmatically flexible according to the situation and times, conforms to self-imposed high standards of public conduct. Once practically interchangeable with 'moral', this term has acquired quasi-legal connotations and has moved closer to 'legitimate' following the recent (2nd half of 20th century) schism between private morality and public morality. So, while considering morality, we have to consider public morality and legitimacy as per laws of the land.

Every business survives only till it is profitable. However, an ethically-oriented culture is one where final financial results do matter but not at the cost of ethics, morals, values and legal compliances. Such organizations never take their sights off the greater good of nature, society or mankind. An organization that emphasizes ethical behaviour at all times will emphasize doing the right thing even when it is costly. Unethical behaviours in such organizations are treated with highest levels of punishment.

Communications in companies with ethical orientation are highly transparent and everyone, irrespective of one's level in hierarchy, is heard when it comes to matters of what is ethically right or wrong. So, decisions can always be challenged if some employee feels that the particular decision is morally or ethically not right.

In such company cultures, customers as well as employees are considered very important partners in business. Employees get their due welfare, training and growth opportunities, though it is not very highly emphasized as happens in people-oriented culture.

People - Oriented Culture

Richard Branson has famously said – "Clients do not come first, employees come first. If you take care of your employees, they will take care of the clients." He also said - "Take care of your employees and they will take care of your business. It's as simple as that."

People-oriented companies recognize that all employees, no matter how big or small their roles, are vital contributors to the success of the company. Employees are treated and respected accordingly as valued partners and it is a culture of mutual respect. Such businesses make employee's success and growth a central priority. In these companies, a lot of stress is given on training and promoting internal talent.

In people-oriented companies, customer service also gets due importance. The two are seen as inextricably linked i.e. when employees are happy and take pride in their jobs, they naturally would want to make their customers and clients happy.

In such businesses, due importance is given to values, ethics, corporate governance and company processes. Interpersonal behaviours are defined by mutual respect, justice, fairness, trust, integrity and accountability.

Communication are transparent, and employees are explained why of decision-making and employees are involved in decision-making. Management integrity is high in such cultures and leaders are role models. One generally finds that top-management of such companies would have generally risen from junior-most levels in the same company.

Culture of Contradictions

Oxford Dictionary defines 'contradiction' as a combination of statements, ideas or features which are opposed to one another. It also defines it as 'a situation in which inconsistent elements are present'.

> *An extreme case of 'culture od contradictions' is the now defunct 'Enron'. Sims and Brinkman (2003) described Enron's ethics as" the ultimate contradiction between words and deeds, between a deceiving glossy façade and a rotten structure behind" (p. 243). Enron executives flashed valued and ethics as the cornerstone of their business but prioritized profits over ethical behaviour and what is right i.e. whatever they claimed or branded themselves as, didn't truly exist.*

Deriving from the definitions of the words culture and contradiction, a 'Culture of Contradictions' is one where the claimed, branded or perceived values or behaviours or ethical standards or processes in an organization or a part of it are different from the actual practiced ones.

In multinational corporations, there are always subcultures within the overarching company culture propagated and aspired by the top-most management or shareholders. There may be cases where the company seeks to establish an ethically-oriented culture in the entire company but a subculture in a subsidiary in another geography has a profit-oriented culture. This might happen because of a particular leader or communication-gap between the corporate office and the subsidiary or wrong short-term priorities at either level or misalignment of values and strategy etc.

> *Between 2013 and 2015, the Wall Street Journal had reported that Walmart paid millions of dollars in bribes in India, China, Brazil and Mexico. Even Walmart corporate headquarters had conducted internal investigations into these allegations. A few members of senior management in India operations were removed afterwards. So, effectively in spite of Walmart trying to convey an image of being ethical and legally compliant, there were cultural contradictions.*

For assessing 'culture of contradictions', there can be various parameters such as communication styles where a company can claim to be open in communication and one promoting two-way communication but in actual practice there is one-way communication from top-to-bottom levels. Another such case can be one where a company claims to be people-oriented with focus on talent-retention and growth but rarely promotes people internally and their human resources departments are always busy hiring talent from outside.

While observing cultural types or patterns in an organization, there are two important aspects that need to be looked into i.e. consistency between the organization claimed cultural type and practiced one; and if there are contradictions, how serious the contradictions are and more so for the parameters which are important for oneself. We must always observe these critical parameters and analyse them more intensely for our job-security, career progression, job-satisfaction, work-life balance, self-conscience dilemmas and most important of all crucial personal decision-making.

Such contradictions generally arise from personality types and priorities of top leadership of such subsidiaries. There can be many manifestations of 'culture of contradictions' and it is very important for us to understand such contractions and the degree of contradictions i.e. how serious and pronounced the contradictions are.

We need to know, understand and be consciously aware of the real culture prevalent in our organization because on the face of it, every organization claims and tries to project itself as an ethical and employee-oriented profit-making business.

Judging other organization's culture

This brings us to another important topic which is – judging other organization's cultures and should we judge others? A lot of factors must have contributed to the forming of and later continuing culture in an organization because similar to changing an existing culture, forming a culture can't happen overnight. If a culture has been formed and sustained itself in an organization, then should we be judging it as an outsider? The very fact that a culture has sustained over a period of time in an organization implies that it has met some purposes either for the organization or for those who helped sustain it, especially senior management or promoters.

In Anthropology, ethnocentrism refers to using our culture as the centre and evaluating other cultures based on it. On the other hand, cultural relativism refers to not judging a culture to our standards of what is right or wrong, strange or normal. Anthropologists say that when we think about different cultures and societies, we should think about their customs in ways that helps us make sense of how their cultural practices fit with their overall cultural context.

Can the same be said about organizational cultures i.e. does ethnocentrism exist among professionals in work-life and should cultural relativism be the norm?

Ethnocentrism in Organizational Context

In organizational context, ethnocentrism would refer to using our organization's culture or our moral and ethical values and principles as the centre and evaluating other cultures based on it.

> *Tez has always worked in an MNC and he generally talked derogatively about culture existing in every owner driven company. Saz had never worked in an MNC and always dreamt about working in one because he perceived that every MNC has a better working culture.*

We find a lot of examples around us wherein we or our colleagues talk derogatively or appreciatively about our perception of existing cultures in other organizations. Is it really warranted or even true? Think of a situation wherein an owner in a owner-driven company is someone who believes in justice and employee growth and though there are no written policies, yet the culture develops around the owner's beliefs. Whereas in a subsidiary of an MNC, there exists a Culture of Contradictions, which is the most dangerous place to work at. What happens if professionals takes career decisions based on the preconceived ideas about organizational cultures?

Cultural Relativism in Organizational Context

This is where the concept of cultural relativism becomes important in thinking about or assessing organizational cultures. Similar to anthropologists, when we think about different cultures and organizations, we should think about their customs in a way that helps us make sense of how their cultural practices fit with their overall cultural context and organizational types.

For example, a start-up has to focus completely on making the business sustainable first because if that happens, then only the business will survive, else why every government provides tax relief to start-ups. Whereas, well-established older company can and should think of other important parameters such as company processes and their strict adherence, corporate governance, contributing in corporate social responsibility etc. and develop culture around these parameters.

However, cultural relativism should only be used as a tool to develop better understanding about other cultures as well as the culture existing in our organization. This concept doesn't provide an alibi to us or others to justify a 'culture of contradictions' or an 'unethical culture' that some of us might have created or are trying to create.

For us, as consciously aware professionals, it is very important that we don't follow an 'ethnocentric' approach by having preconceived notions or prejudices about organizational cultures from the standpoint of our ethical or moral principles or from the standpoint of our organization's culture. Following an ethnocentric approach is similar to us wanting to be happy only if everything happens as per our wishes.

We shouldn't be ethnocentric while trying to understand our or other organizational culture. We also need to understand the culture in an organization as it exists and assess whether our personality and behaviour is or will be in sync with that culture type. This understanding and conscious awareness about an organization's culture and our synergy or dissonance with that culture enables us to guide our behaviours and actions to bring synergy and conscientious decision-making, if there are no possibilities of bringing synergies. For this, knowing our organization objectively at a deeper level is important.

11. Knowing Our Organization

"The stranger sees only what he knows." – African Proverb

This African proverb rightly summarises an important aspect of human perception i.e. unconsciously but primarily we pay attention to only those elements of an organizational culture that we are familiar with. As a consciously aware professional, we must attempt to look at all related cultural aspects than trying to form perception about culture of our organization on one or two parameters.

Every organization is a unique entity in itself and can be at any stage of its dynamic developmental stage. This uniqueness is a result of various factors such as ownership, management, aging, size, geographical spread and at what level of growth a company is, at any given point of time. Also, it is important to keenly observe, understand and be consciously aware of the impact of the organizational type on the work culture as well as on leadership behaviour.

To understand and know our organizational culture and bringing about conscious awareness of the same, we need to look deeper into our organization and know it at an objective level. This helps us in assessing whether our personality is in sync with the organizational culture of the organization we are working at and also assessing paradoxical situations and behaviours of some colleagues or leaders.

For knowing our organizational culture at an objective level, we need to list-out parameters which are important for us, according to our personality. These parameters will vary from one professional to another and are the ones which, consciously or unconsciously, set our expectations from the organization. For example, as a Hercules professional, we may expect and be in sync with a highly ethical, process-oriented culture where there is accountability for actions; whereas as a Mercenary or Hypocrite, we may expect and be in sync with a culture with less focus on strict ethical standards, process-orientation and accountability or responsibility.

Though these parameters can vary from one professional to another, yet some common parameters can help us in objectively assessing and knowing our organization and its culture.

Employee-Related Parameters

Employee-related parameters help us in knowing as to how we as employees, in general, view the organization as well as how we are viewed in the organization by management and leadership. It helps us understand if the organizational culture is employee-oriented or not.

How long employees stay?

How long employees, in general, stay in the organization helps us understand the organizational culture at a deeper level. A longer stay and growth of employees, reaching top management levels during this stay, points to an employee-friendly organizational culture which values it employees.

However, sometimes this may also happen because the organization has matured, expanded and reached MNC level. Then, the organization brings-in HRD policy of inducting management trainees for later leadership roles. These management trainees over a period of time move into leadership roles far more quickly than anticipated in normal course. In such a scenario, if we are not a management trainee, we must remember at all times that this group of employees, i.e. the management trainees who entered year-after-year, will always identify more with each other than with others. They will always get preference over outsiders for promotions and leadership roles.

We also needs to be conscious of this parameter in the context of junior, middle or senior management levels and which level one is working at. For example, the organization explained above might see employees at junior and mid-levels staying longer with well-deserved promotions. Subsequently, those mid-level managers not be able to rise to senior levels owing to the places being filled by management trainees turned leaders. In such a scenario, in spite of well-published HRD policies, a non-management trainee or an outsider middle-management level professional may not or very rarely reach senior-levels in such organizations.

If we are in the above situation, it is advisable for us to switch organization to grow beyond middle-management level. If we are in such a situation and not a management trainee, it is always wise to use the brand and the platform to move to some higher role in another organization where this differentiation doesn't exist, else we are always likely to be unsatisfied with the situation. On the other hand, if we are one of those management trainees, we must try to stay in the same organization as long as possible because we will get best growth avenues in this very organization.

Overall, we need to be consciously aware of this parameter and keenly observe and assess it very objectively vis-à-vis our position and expectations.

The Strongest Reason for Stay

If our organization has employees who are staying longer than expected, even without getting growth opportunities, one needs to delve deeper into the reasons.

Is *'brand image'* the only glue making employees continue? If yes, it is more likely to happen in case of MNCs. Do we think maximum of such employees will leave if they are offered employment elsewhere with similar or slightly less famous brand? If yes, the organizational culture of that MNC or its subsidiary needs to be more keenly observed to understand it. Is it the *'loyalty to the company'* owing to job security that the company has provided to its employees over a longer period of time? It is more likely to happen in case of owner driven companies which have grown at a regular pace and retained their employees consciously as a policy.

This parameter again helps us understand and know our organization and to understand the probability of being in sync or not with the organization's culture. If we get motivated more by prestige and for whom brand matters a lot, we will prefer an MNC with strong brand irrespective of culture at a deeper level; whereas if we are looking for stable career over a longer period of time will prefer the later organization, described above.

Promotions – from within or recruited from outside

Are employees from within organization given preference, or not, over fresh recruitments for promotions? This is one of the most important parameters for us to understand culture of our company. We shouldn't blindly believe in our company's publicized policies of adhering to 'performance based promotion culture' but keenly observe this parameter.

This parameter has the maximum effect on our happiness and career- growth in an organization and we need to be conscious of actual situation instead of expecting a result which is in contrast to our observations. For example, if we observed that there were vacancies published on company's website but every time instead of promoting well-deserving talent from within the company, outside recruitments happened, then in such a company, even if we are most suitable for a future position, that is going to be vacant, should we expect our selection?

Being consciously aware of this parameter helps us keep our expectations to a realistic level and avoid unhappy situations for ourselves.

Perception about Ex-employees

This parameter speaks a lot about the organizational culture of a company i.e. whether the culture is healthy and positive or it is toxic and negative. Are employees who left the company spoken about positively and appreciated for the good work they did during their journey with the company or vilified in general and blamed for everything that is going wrong in the company at present?

In case we are working in the former type of organization, we can be rest assured that we will have a journey which will be self-satisfying and we will treasure the memories for rest of our life. In case, we observe the later trend in our organization i.e. employees and leaders speaking negatively about predecessors or ex-employees, whatever good we may do, we will neither leave the organization as a satisfied and contented employee norwe will see this tenure enhancing our reputation in the market once we have moved on. Our successors and ex-colleagues will keep speaking negative about us as long as they can.

Leadership-Related Parameters

The below listed parameters provide an insight into the leadership and decision-making style of our organization. Being conscious and knowing the same help us understand the wider organizational culture because leadership team provides a glimpse into the existing culture as well as direction of the future cultural changes.

Integrity of Leadership

When we talk about leadership in this context, it refers to all or majority of the managers and leaders as a group. How do we assess integrity of a group of leaders? It is by keenly observing the behaviour patterns of the leaders in the company.

We need to be observant of behaviours such as, do the leaders share credit for success with the teams; do the leaders take responsibility for wrong decisions or team failures or blame team-members for the same; are the leaders trying to keep their word on most of the occasions i.e. not changing stand every now and then; do the leaders behave and conduct as role-models displaying unbiased, honest, justice-oriented, ethical behaviours; are majority of leaders ensuring legal compliances and adhering to laws of the land?

If the answers to above questions is positive for majority of leaders, then the organization has ethical culture in general and the same is displayed in behaviours of the leaders and the few who may not be doing so don't identify with the organizational culture. However, if the answer is negative for majority of leaders including the top-most leader in the hierarchy, then it represents an unethical culture. This may happen irrespective of the company policies being in existence or not. However, if the company prescribes ethical policies and still the unethical culture is in place, then paradox is a case of culture of contradictions.

Decision-making Process

We must observe if the leadership team is taking logical decisions and whenever team-members don't understand logic of a decision, are they allowed to ask relevant question or they are supposed to just follow the decisions. Are employees encouraged to ask questions or hounded passively if they ask questions? This parameter helps us understand as to what kind of organization we are working-in i.e. a top-down, closed-door decision-making type where employee's opinions aren't valued or open, logical decision-making type where employees as well as their opinions are valued.

This will further help us understand and assess the probability of our personality being in sync or not with the organization we are working with. Also, the degree of dissonance we might be experiencing or are likely to experience can also be understood using this parameter.

Top and Bottom Three Rule

How do we find-out if the senior-most leader of our company, subsidiary or business or our manager has a sense of justice and honesty or has strong personal biases while treating employees? Each one of us may not be in direct contact with our top leader such as Country Head for middle and senior management employees or senior management for junior and middle-management employees. However, we must have been observing his/her next line of leaders and similarly our colleagues must have been doing so.

Based on common perception about leaders in the company, who are the three top performing and three bottom performing next-line leaders? Having known that, we must observe - does the top leader have at least two of the top-performing next line leaders in his/ her inner coterie and are they given preferential treatment in promotions or decision-making of the company? If yes, he believes in justified actions. Alternatively, does the top leader have two of the worst performing next-line leaders in his/her coterie, getting preferential treatment and even promotions, at times? If yes, he/she has a biased sense of justice.

Why this parameter is important for us to understand? The senior-most leader impacts the culture of an organization in a major way because his next levels and their next levels tend to follow the top leader, unless they have strong personality-related differences with the leader. Most of the times, teams consciously or unconsciously follow the top leader and his/her behaviour and working style is copied by majority of other leaders and employees.

Reasons of Employees Leaving the Organization

There may be several reasons why employees leave the organization. However, we need to carefully observe as to how many left or were asked to leave because of difference of opinion with their managers, irrespective of levels? Such forced resignations might have been camouflaged as leadership issue or something else but vast majority of employees are always aware of the overt as well as covert reasons.

If we find that majority of employees, who left the organization, were the ones who had major differences with their managers, then it indicates a culture with absence of openness, process-oriented policies or their execution, values and ethics in the organization. Such organizations have strong perception-forming culture and managers are more often busy creating biased perception against those employees who don't fall in line, so that they can be forced to exit. Such managers are busy plotting and planning these actions and lose focus on task at hand.

This type of unethical culture can be present in any type of organization irrespective of publicized policies, ownership or geography. This is a result of either owners promoting such cultures or Country Heads, with specific personality types, promoting such cultures in their area of influence in MNCs, irrespective of the global policies of those MNCs.

A conscious awareness about such culture and our level of acceptance of such cultural practices helps us in conscious decision-making.

Culture-Related Parameters

In addition to the above parameters, below listed culture related parameters provide subtle hints the prevalent culture in an organization and we need to be conscious of these parameters while judging our organization and its working culture.

Are employees at different levels treated differently?

When we talk of rules being different for levels, it implies different hierarchical levels being treated differently with respect to training, performance related rewards, allowances or bonuses etc., with the same being cornered by a select few. In our organization, it is important to be consciously aware if hierarchical levels exist only for the sake of job allocation based on skills and experience, or it is more akin to medieval history's feudal system where even an employee's respect, as a human being, depends on his/her hierarchical level?

Does the promoter / owner or the senior-most leader or set of leaders treat employees with respect or as just subjects who are there to obey orders? This can be observed in verbal, non-verbal as well as written communication styles. There are instances where professionals have narrated stories of even junior-most employees being treated with utmost respect by CEOs. At the same time, there are professionals who have been treated by their managers / company-owners / bosses worse than bonded labours of ancient or medieval history. Other cases will be between these two extreme cases.

As professionals, we need to be aware of the above aspect and assess if our expectations from the organization and its culture are in sync with the same.

Responsibility

In an organization, there will always be behaviour patterns and past instances to help us assess the accountability and responsibility matrix and implementation thereof. A common saying is – *'Success has many fathers but failure is always an orphan'*. So, in our organization, we need to assess who owns responsibility for failures? Are the decision-makers, or actual people who should be taking responsibility and held accountable or are lower levels of hierarchy made responsible i.e. scapegoats for failures?

True leaders always distribute the fruits of success among team-members but own responsibility for failures and in the process make sure everyone learns how not to repeat similar failures. A conscious awareness about responsibility-fixing and accountability culture in our organization helps us assess if in spite of putting-in best efforts, will we find ourselves at the receiving end for someone else failure?

Use of Audits

In every organization there are audits of one or other kinds i.e. some statutory audits and some as guided by company's policies and processes. In either case, there are going to be observations. For what purpose does our organization use these audits or observations thereof? These can be used either for correcting whatever has been inadvertently missed-out or for improving the processes or for finding-out if something was done with wrong intention i.e. to hide something or to get benefit from such omission etc. or to settle personal scores or image-building by senior leadership.

The first three uses are the ones for which an audit is carried-out. It is the last type that we need to be careful about because audits can always be used by senior management or leaders to settle personal scores or to present an image of themselves being too honest and compliant. These instances can also happen during cultural transition phase i.e. when changes are being implemented in an organization and culture.

We need to be careful about how audits are being carried-out and for what purposes they are eventually used in our organization.

Values – Reality or Façade?

As a word, 'Values' is most number of times used word in work-places in last two decades when it comes to discussing organizational culture. Now-a-days, it appears as a mention in almost all websites of the corporate organizations, be it of any type and following any culture. A lot of parameters which we have discussed above appear as 'values' in publicized policies of most of the organizations in corporate world. For example, we find mention of words such as integrity, honesty, performance-culture, equal opportunity, adherence to all legal compliances and corporate governance principles, all employee being treated equality irrespective of colour, sex, race, religion, geography etc.

Organizations have varied levels of using the word 'Values'. It varies from finding mention on company website, to having values as a document circulated as a policy, to an attempt being made by corporate headquarters to implement values through training, to actually values being an important part of how business is done in an organization. On the flip-side, there are instances wherein 'values' are used by managers and senior management to get rid of non-confirming team-members by creating a false perception about such team-members and using this as a pretext to forcing exit of team-members who aren't agreeable to such managers or leaders.

As professionals, we must be consciously aware about some of the aspects such as, what is the emphasis level of the word 'values' in our organization; are 'values' guiding principles only or to be followed in letter and spirit; does the top management and senior leadership exhibit behaviours which are in sync with publicized 'values'; is the concept of 'values' being used as a perception creating tool by leaders to get rid of non-confirming team-members and next line of leaders, though majority of their teams don't find anything wrong with behaviours of such team-members.

Our conscious awareness of 'values' being a reality or façade in our organization makes it easier for us to understand if we are working in an ethical culture or a culture of contradictions. This factor assumes more importance if we are working in a Multi-National Company or professionally-managed organization and carrying an impression or perception which is contrary to the real situation on ground. By the time, we realize that our perceptions were contrary to the reality, it might be too late and we may feel even more dejected leading to unhappiness.

*

Knowing our organization's culture through objective observation of various parameters and being consciously aware of its various aspects helps us guide our behaviour and also help us make informed and conscientious decisions at a personal and professional level for the immediate as well as for longer-term.

Apart from helping us in our decision-making, conscious awareness about work culture of our organization impacts our happiness in more than one way. If our personality and the emphasis we have on ethical and moral values in our life are in stark contrast to the work culture of our organization, then we suffer an internal dissonance and lose our peace of mind and most of the times, we aren't able to share the same with anyone.

At the same time, being ignorant and not being conscious of organizational culture of our work-place, we may not even find the reasons behind our unhappiness. Sometimes, in pursuit of being accepted as a team-member or integral part of organizational culture, we take everything as holy truth and we neither analyse the organizational culture nor become conscious of it, even if we analyse the same. This behaviour is similar to being ignorant, automated and unconscious behaviour and we can never be at peace with such a behaviour.

Being consciously aware doesn't imply that we need to react at smallest of the dissonances. On the other hand, our conscious awareness should act as an enabler in our conscious transformation and conscientious decision-making, when we become aware that even transformation may not result in harmony, peace and happiness.

12. Cultural Synergies

"You have to maintain a culture of transformation and stay true to your values." – Jeff Weiner

To feel happy and grow personally and professionally, we must remain open to the idea of transforming ourselves by adapting to new ways of thinking and behaving. However, this can be a dilemma for us when our values and ethical principles may not be in sync with that of our organizational culture. Each one of us need to objectively assess how true this perceived dissonance is.

Having known our organization, its type and culture by objectively looking deeper at various parameters, which are important to us and how things happen on a daily basis, it becomes equally important to find-out and be self-conscious if we are in sync with the working culture of our organization or not. A lot of times, even being competent and ethical professionals, we may not succeed because we may not be at the right place i.e. an organization where our values are in sync with organizational culture. As a consciously aware professional, we must strive to find-out what does the organization actually value and assessing the synergy between those actually practiced organizational values and our values.

Below three true stories (names changed) will help us in understanding what is meant by being in sync or not being in sync with our organizational culture.

Cultural Story - 1

Ravi was ethical, honest, upright and upfront professional with excellent academic and professional credentials. He was someone who led from front and his team respected him a lot, both as a leader and person. He was highly conscious of the legal compliances and corporate governance principles and followed them in letter and spirit. He joined an Indian Subsidiary of a MNC, which commanded a great brand value in the market. While working in the organization at middle-management level and later at senior management level, he observed that everyone, including Indian Leadership, spoke highly of values, ethical practices, and transparency in working, decision-making and valuing its employees along with following legal and corporate governance principles. Ravi thought he had landed-up at a right place in his career and his personality is in sync with the organizational culture.

However, with passing time over the years and specially within a year of him becoming part of the senior management team of the Indian subsidiary, , he started realizing that he was in a 'culture of contradictions' i.e. all the talks of high values, employee growth and welfare, ethics, legal compliances etc. were merely for speaking.

He observed that the leadership of this Indian subsidiary had created a wall of opaqueness between their teams and overseas Headquarters and whatever Indian leaders said or presented was believed to be true. CEOs of the Indian subsidiary considered the place as their fiefdom and they had their own coterie of senior management people, who got preferred treatment irrespective of their capabilities.

CEOs were more interested in taking-out old-time employees who were more loyal to the brand and instead of promoting from within, recruitments from outside were preferred because the new entrants are always more likely to be loyal to the person who recruited them *than being loyal to the brand. Legal compliances or corporate governance principles got importance only on paper else they flouted environmental, financial or competition laws of the land to achieve financial targets. The culture was one of every leader and manager trying to corner accolades for little success and blaming teams down-below, predecessors or other colleagues for all the failures.*

Was Ravi at a right place i.e. was he a cultural fit or misfit? Ravi was a Hercules professional who valued hard-work, performance-driven, ethical and employee-oriented culture. His organization propagated and claimed to be a performance-driven, ethical, employee-oriented culture. So, effectively his decision to join this subsidiary was right as his values and those propagated by the organization at global level were in sync.

However, in actual practice he was working in a subsidiary of that larger organization and this subsidiary had a sub-culture which was a 'culture of contradictions'. There was a complete disconnect between overall organizational culture and culture of this subsidiary. Therefore, as a consciously aware professional, Ravi must be aware of these three aspects i.e. his values, organizational values and values actually practiced in the subsidiary that he working with.

Simply being aware of this disconnect or dissonance may not be of much help unless Ravi is consciously aware and is able to make-out if he can make adjustments in his expectations regarding what kind of organization he should be working at and take decisions if those transformations aren't of much help. As said in the beginning of chapter, Ravi should be open to the idea of transforming himself provided he doesn't lose his basic personality and values in the process.

Cultural Story – 2

Mohit had joined a start-up in the early part of his career. This start-up was started by a young, enthusiastic entrepreneur who wanted to become profitable and grow as soon as possible. It had been 2 years since this business started when Mohit joined it. The owner and Mohit were in their twenties with Mohit being 5 years younger. He did a great work for and with his owner and the business grew manifold in next 10 years. Mohit was recognized in the company and also outside among customers as bright young professional who can make things happen.

By this time, Mohit had gained personality traits of Mercenary Personality, who could make things happen but at the cost of legal compliances and corporate governance principles. There was great influence on his work personality of the organizational culture and working environment of the start-up as well as of the entrepreneur that he worked with. He couldn't and didn't learn the importance of following legal compliances or corporate governance principles in this organization. On the contrary, he unconsciously learnt that overlooking these compliances while achieving the larger financial goal of company is normal and there is nothing wrong in doing so.

Mohit got an opportunity to work for a MNC and he jumped at the prospect of working in an MNC corporate culture. It was his dream to work for this company while he was still in his Engineering College. He joined at middle-management level with lot of excitement and expectations. However, the excitement seemed to be short-lived for him. He was in turmoil because in spite of delivering much higher than his committed targets, he was time and again being counselled regarding small legal compliances (as he perceived them to be) that he didn't follow.

He was counselled by his manager regarding his ways of working. Mohit pointed out that the manager himself had said he wanted the *task to be completed at any cost, why he was counseling him now. Mohit argued that he didn't do such a big crime by paying a small facilitation fee to the government official, which is a norm in the industry. Also, he had been doing it for last 10 years in his previous company and there was no issue whatsoever. Mohit's manager told him that in this company you need to achieve everything within rules and regulations.*

Mohit wasn't able to comprehend much during these conversations or counselling sessions and from a high performing team-member, he withdrew to becoming an unhappy passenger, doing his routine job with no enthusiasm.

Was Mohit at a right place i.e. was his work personality in cultural sync with his new organization's culture? Though Mohit was a hard-working, competent professional but owing to his initial work-life exposure, he had developed a Mercenary personality wherein he got used to exceeding targets at the cost of ethics, values and government compliances. Without understanding the difference in organizational cultures of his previous organization and new organization, he continued working with similar set of values. He was at a right place with wrong set of values as a baggage from his previous experience.

As a consciously aware professional, Mohit should be aware of his personality, behaviour traits, strengths and weaknesses and where he stands on principles of values, ethics, integrity, morality, willingness or not to be legally compliant and what will make him satisfied and happy i.e. knowing himself at deeper level is very important. He must be also aware of his organization's actual culture and must always be ready to transform himself for the better.

Cultural Story – 3: Cultural Paradox

John had hardly spent 3 years in this company which was an industry leader and had been in India for quite some time. During these three years, he had heard numerous stories from those employees who were instrumental in setting-up the Indian subsidiary. Nalin had once narrated – "To establish this company in India, we used to distribute facilitation charges to various stakeholders to make sure operations are smooth. In fact managers used to pass fake bills to cover such transactions." On another occasion, Sharma, who had been in company for a very long time, had told – "I can't believe this company talking about compliances and blaming old-time employees. I have seen two briefcases full of high currency notes being taken by overseas team-members, who went to meet ministry officials." So, this was what the old time employees had seen as far as this company's culture was concerned.

During second decade of twenty first century, the legal and compliance related pressure on MNCs was increasing globally and heavy fines were being imposed on companies apart from legal actions against their top managements. Monetary fines is the best language which commercial organizations understand. Ideally, this organization should have been legally compliant at all times but it didn't happen. So, instead of taking proactive steps while it was expanding in various geographies, a compliance culture at global level was set rolling, as a reaction to the global compliance norms.

John could see the visible unease which old-time employees were feeling at all these changes and the transition phase in culture. Unease was not because they didn't want to be legally and statutorily compliant but it was because the new management and compliance heads were trying to become hero by pointing-out older irregularities, though these very people were looking the other way till some time back. The old-time employees at senior and middle management levels felt that they can be made scapegoats by these *compliance heads to score brownie points. It did happen in a few cases.*

This cultural paradox, and a feeling of not being at the right place i.e. not being culturally in sync anymore, can happen to professionals who have been staying in an organization for longer period. Owing to new strict legal provisions and monetary fines at international levels, a lot of MNCs are emphasizing change in cultures from one of overlooking compliances to being completely compliant at country as well as international level. In such companies, there is a transition happening.

Such cultural transitions can be very painful for old-time employees, who have learnt to work in a certain way in that company and its culture and are now being blamed or counselled regularly to follow everything in letter and spirit. These employees feel that whatever they did, in the past, was for company's benefit and as to why they are being blamed now. Such employees have been working in a certain organizational culture and were completely in sync with organization's culture and when there is a transition happening, they feel themselves to be cultural misfits.

*

As consciously aware professionals, we must understand that commercial organizations are not living entities and loyalty to organization should never take priority over being legally compliant and following laws of the land. The leaders who looked the other way, when we might have been doing wrong things for helping the organization, will either refuse knowing the same or leave for greener pastures.

It is always important to understand whether we are at a right place or not i.e. whether we are is in sync with our organizational culture or not. Apart from our manager and colleagues, organizational culture determines the way things are happening in present and will happen in future in this particular organization where we are working. Even behaviour of our colleagues, managers and leaders get impacted by organizational culture. So knowing, whether we are culturally in sync or not, also helps determine the reasons for likely dissonance with colleagues or managers and resulting unhappiness for us as well as others.

Such knowledge of being or not being in sync also helps us decide on the probability of reaching a stage of being in sync and feeling happy, if we make subtle changes in our behaviour. The decision to make these subtle changes must be a conscious one knowing the likely end-results. This knowledge helps us draw lines as to how much we are willing to change in order to be in sync and happy with organizational culture. The steps that we intend to take shouldn't result in inner turmoil and disturbing our peace of mind due to vast differences between our existing values and how we want to behave to bring synergies with an organizational culture.

Can those of us who have very high standards of ethics, morals, integrity and honesty make sufficient changes to be in sync with organizational culture of an organization and remain happy where unethical means are the norm? Or else those of us who have always worked by overlooking ethical and honest way of working to achieve personal goals, sustain in an ethical organization which runs on high standards of ethics, morals, values of integrity and honesty?

So, effectively, this knowledge of being in sync or not being in sync with our organization not only helps us make professional decisions in life but also helps make conscientious personal decisions in work-life.

13. Being Consciously Aware

"Remember that your perception of the world is a reflection of your state of consciousness." – Eckhart Tolle

We are in a state of happiness when what we think, what we say and what we do are in harmony and reaching that state of happiness is possible if we bring all the facets of conscious awareness together. It will helps us perceive all dimensions of work-life with more knowledge, understanding and awareness and also helps us in understanding and being aware of our synergies or dissonances and reasons thereof. What we should be desiring is not being happy but feeling happy because being happy is a momentary thing whereas feeling happy is a journey and can stretch as long as we are consciously aware.

Each one of us feel happy or unhappy with certain kind of managers or work-cultures and we must be consciously aware of those combinations. Our awareness will enable us in limiting our expectations from unfavourable combinations. These lowered expectations and better understanding will make us feel happy even in situations where we might be experiencing dissonance because we are aware of inevitability or likelihood such dissonances.

Let us discuss where do we, as professionals with our personality, have maximum synergy and where we might experience maximum dissonances i.e. with which type of manager and organization do we find maximum synergies or dissonances? Being consciously aware of our personality type enables us to work on areas of improvement and subtle changes to our behaviour to bring more synergies and happiness in our work-life.

Hercules Personality

Those of us with Hercules personality at a junior and middle-management level, we find maximum synergies in an organization with ethical and process-oriented culture such as a Start-up by professionals or MNCs, with our manager being a Hercules or Aristotle type. In these situations, we will generally find ourselves happy and satisfied with our work productivity as well as career growth being at the best possible levels.

As senior level professionals, we will be most productive with an Aristotle CEO and may also be more or less satisfied with a Hercules and sometimes with a Professor CEO, if the CEO is suave, polished and follows ethical standards and also legal compliances.

As far as organizational culture is concerned, the most suitable culture for us is only an ethical, process-oriented and employee-oriented culture. For us, the most positive aspect is that we are always accepted as true leaders, highly regarded and respected by our teams. We will find that our teams are emotionally connected to us.

However, as consciously aware Hercules professionals, we need to take special care of some important aspects such as, improving our emotional quotient and not reacting in person or in mails; not expressing our opinions till asked for; identifying colleagues who tend to feed us with inputs which result in emotional outbursts and being careful of these colleagues by only listening to them and not reacting.

We must be consciously aware that change is the only constant in life and therefore we shouldn't get emotionally attached to company, task or team-members because we aren't going to be in the same work set-up for our entire life. Shrewd managers will tend to use other's hard-work and emotions for their advantage without looking after their interests. As Hercules professionals, we need to be careful of such managers. At the same time, true leaders will use such skill-set and personality traits positively and also guide Hercules professionals so that they can also progress. We must try being with such leaders for the maximum part of our work-life.

Irrespective of our personality type, if we are in a leadership position and we find a team-member with herculean personality traits, we must remember such team-members are our best assets. We must use them judiciously and honestly and guide them positively by helping them improve their emotional quotient. We need to remember that no one is perfect in this world so it helps us as well as organization, if we avoid their occasional emotional outbursts and keep them on a right path. If such team-member are successful, we are successful.

At senior or leadership levels, we as Hercules professionals have two serious concern areas in our professional life; first being, synergy with our manager i.e. CEO, MD etc. and second, our emotional nature. A conscious awareness of this synergy / dissonance issue and emotional behaviour trait and working positively towards overcoming these two concern areas can contribute positively towards our professional success, personal satisfaction and happiness in professional life.

In view of our likely dissonance with our managers which may be at CEO levels, we need to be consciously aware that

CEOS who aren't Hercules or Aristotle themselves experience dissonance while working with Hercules tem-members. Such managers may scheme or plot against us by turning our team-members against us and with the help of such team-members, they can create a distorted perception that we, as leaders, are autocrat. Those team-members of ours who display personality traits of being free-rider, hypocrite or parasite are the one who have strong dissonance with us. These are the team-members who are likely to help, the CEO or colleagues of the Hercules senior professional, in creating the false perception through gossips and talking derogatively to hide their own non-contribution. This distorted perception causes maximum damage to the image and professional career of ours i.e. a Hercules senior management professional, as our leadership and team loyalty is biggest asset.

At times, the goal-achievement by us as Hercules leaders can be used against us by our manager, who creates a perception of us as being mercenaries. A CEO will do so by unnecessarily over-highlighting small audit objections as a consistent non-compliant behaviour of the Hercules leader.

Therefore, as a Hercules senior level professional, we must be consciously aware of not only our dissonance with our manager i.e. the CEO and the office politics that CEO might be playing but also team-members who display behaviour traits of Hypocrite, Free Rider and Parasite Personality types because such team-members will be catalysts in creating the distorted perception.

A conscious awareness of the above synergies, own strengths, improvement areas and likely dissonances will enable a Hercules professional to perceive work-life more realistically and make conscious decisions to transform oneself for inner and outer harmony, happiness and growth.

Aristotle Personality

At a junior or even middle management level, as Aristotle professionals, we must try and choose consulting or related career options to optimally utilize our higher knowledge and ability to think at strategic or macro-level. If we are working in a hierarchical organization with strict job-roles, we will do better staying closer to the senior-most management members in roles such as executive assistant to CEO or planning-related roles and helping senior-management. Through these roles, we can help by fresh ideas and learning in the process and letting the time pass till senior management realizes presence of higher mental abilities in us and utilizes our talent accordingly.

In a middle-management role, we are most productive when working with a Hercules or Aristotle manager because such managers are able to harness the knowledge and higher thought process of Aristotle middle management professionals and utilize the same in very constructive manner for the business goals.

As Aristotle senior professionals, we are the best fit in senior management roles, as we can provide a macro view of the business, provide strategy and guide or mentor our team-members. After providing a strategy or direction, we must take a backseat and let our teams do the task. In senior management roles, we are the favourite team-members for CEOs with Aristotle, Hercules or Passenger personalities because all other personality type CEOs perceive Aristotle senior management professionals as overconfident and arrogant about their knowledge and trying to falsely present a calm and composed personality.

At all levels of hierarchy, we, as Aristotle professionals, prefer working in organizations with ethical process-oriented and legally-compliant culture, irrespective of ownership, size or geography. Also, we tend to find highest levels of dissonance in unethical organizational cultures or cultures of contradiction or in those where leadership isn't clear about the way forward with regard to direction or strategy.

Professor Personality

As professor professionals, we need to know and understand that we are basically very extrovert and must focus on developing the fine art of suave and polished conversations while interacting. We must reduce our speaking time and increasing listening time while in a conversation. We must try and make sure that we are in a customer-facing role at all times. It helps to be consciously aware that no one on this earth is omniscient so it is alright if we don't know something. Accepting it and keeping quite instead of talking irrelevant things is always beneficial to us as professionals.

We need to be consciously aware of our extrovert behaviour trait and how this trait affects others in the team or organization. Over-talking or giving opinions on every subject, situation or colleague can make us quite unpopular in the team leading to unnecessary dissonance. Also, we are prone to inadvertently reveal our lack of knowledge, or depth thereof, due to over-talkative nature and in the process, harm ourselves professionally.

In view of the above, for us, our conscious awareness about ourselves or lack of it, is the biggest factor impacting our professional life instead of our synergies or dissonances or organizational culture of the organization, we are working with.

The other one or two dominant personality traits (other than Professor Personality), which we possess, also impacts us a lot because those additional traits determine our ethical, work-ethics, compliance-related traits and consequent synergies or dissonances with our managers or organizational culture. So, as professionals with professor and Hercules traits, we will exhibit completely different behaviours compared to professionals with professor and free rider personality traits.

If we get to manage professionals with Professor Personality traits, we can get the best business results from such professionals in customer-facing roles only. These professionals can be big failures in desk-roles or operations roles where the focus is more on actual action than on soft-skills or verbal skills.

Passenger Personality

We, as Passenger Personality professionals at junior or middle management levels, display good synergies with our colleagues and managers irrespective of the cultures except in organizations where existing cultures can be best described as opposite of employee-oriented culture. This happens owing to the fact that we prefer a predictable, time-bound and job-clarity kind of working environment.

At a junior or middle level, once we become consciously aware of this dominant personality type in our behaviour, we ought to work in MNCs or Owner-managed larger organizations where job-security is the cultural norm. It is advisable that in the process of working in such organizations with job-security culture, we must upgrade our skill-set to at least the minimum required according to experience in number of years, so that we aren't considered a drag on the organization during later part of our career.

At junior or middle management levels, we also need to be conscious of the fact that sometimes this behaviour trait of being a passenger personality type may result in complacency towards our job converting us from passenger to free rider personality. Also, such complacency makes us susceptible to not being consciously aware of, over-looking or being oblivious of organizational changes which might result in restructuring related job cuts. We must always be consciously aware of such organizational developments in our organization and change organization before we are asked to leave.

It is always a challenge for us to get promotions or leadership roles because very often, the laid back nature of ours goes against us and no one wants to take a risk by putting such people in leadership roles who don't take extra initiative or lead in team-tasks or extra efforts to contribute more than what is expected from them.

In spite of the above, if we, as Passenger professionals, reach senior levels, then we generally share good synergies with our teams, colleagues and managers in Owner-driven large organizations and MNCs. At senior levels, we may be biggest misfits in owner-driven small organizations or start-ups cultures characterized by need for everyone to put-in extra efforts, take extra initiative and where there is ambiguity with respect to CEO or owner's personal behaviour with senior management team-members, job-allocations, accountability, responsibility, organizational strategy etc.

We, as Passenger professionals at all levels, need to be extra careful with being utilized by Mercenaries or Hypocrite

Managers, Leaders or CEOs while such managers indulge in legally non-compliant activities to pursue their short-term goals because more often we are the easiest targets to be made scapegoats if these legally non-compliant activities come to light.

To summarize, being Passenger personality, we are consciously aware of what we need from our job i.e. for us, a job is just an economic activity to support our family. But, we also need to be consciously aware of the work culture of our organization as well as personality traits of our managers and likely impact of both these factors on ourselves and our job security.

Mercenary Personality

We can observe that such professionals at junior and middle levels are able to hide their mercenary behaviours due to their hard-work, soft-skills and nature of agreeing to everything that their manager says. This camouflage helps them have good synergies with colleagues and managers irrespective of organizational culture or type based on ownership, geography etc.

However, as such professionals rise in hierarchy, their true personality of being a mercenary becomes more pronounced as their behaviour of over-achieving business goals irrespective of legal compliances become visible to their colleagues, managers, other senior management professionals or CEOs. However, such professionals are best fit in organizations with profit-oriented, unethical culture with no processes and where top management is willing to overlook anything for profits. Except Hercules and Aristotle managers, mercenary professionals have good synergies with all other managers.

Without sounding to be ethnocentric, it is safe to say that irrespective of society, geography or country, a Mercenary personality type and related behaviours aren't appropriate from any angle, be it moral, ethical, legal, business sustainability or personal liability. However, such professionals always seem to working with their falsely claimed high moral grounds which do not confirm to society's norms or laws of the land. A lot of times, a passionate professional becomes a mercenary over a period of time due to factors such as lack of knowledge about the corporate governance principles, legal compliances, processes and lack of conscious awareness about these as well as early success gained due to overlooking all these factors.

A conscious awareness of such behaviour traits in our personality and working towards eliminating the same from our personality can uplift us from a Mercenary type to a Hercules type. This is possible because as mercenary personality, we already possess lot of behaviour traits of Hercules personality such as hard-work, passion for our role and goal-orientation and we only need to work within processes, norms, legal-compliances and corporate governance principles.

In corporate world, mercenary professionals need to be very careful of being utilized by unscrupulous managers for their short-term benefits and later making those very mercenary professionals scapegoats when legal action happens.

Hypocrite, Free Rider and Parasite Personality Type

Observing the probability of synergy with colleagues or managers, it can be safely said that the behaviours exhibited by Hypocrite, Free Rider and Parasite Personality professionals aren't the desirable and appropriate behaviours for any corporate professional, irrespective of hierarchy levels, organization types or cultures. Such behaviours not only bring dissonance for the professionals themselves but also for the teams and organizations they are working with.

However, no work-place has either been or will be an ideal place and we can easily find professionals displaying such behaviours at all levels of hierarchy, in almost all organizations. Major reason of such professionals existing in our organizations, or in work-life general, is that these behaviours are conditional responses of these professionals to work-setting, since such behaviours have been rewarded in the past by some specific managers or organizations to achieve their short-term goals. These behaviour patterns are majorly responsible for the office politics in any organization as the focus of such professionals is to hide or camouflage their non-contribution with other non-productive behaviours.

Notwithstanding the adverse impacts, such professionals are found to be the best survivors in work-life because their basic goal is own survival, even at the cost of others. Leaders generally ignore such professionals instead of confronting them and unscrupulous managers make them part of their plans.

These professionals are best fit in larger organizations which emphasize collaboration but have unethical culture or culture of contradictions. In such larger organizations, it is easier for them to hide their non-contribution for longer periods of time as there may be plenty others to complete the task. Colleagues of such professionals don't highlight these behaviours as they fear to be perceived as non-collaborative. Without understanding actual meaning of the word 'collaboration', professionals understand it as 'being in agreement to others' and this becomes the best camouflage for such professionals.

These professionals find highest dissonance when working with Hercules managers or in smaller teams or highly goal-focused, ethical, process-oriented organizations where role of every employee is clearly defined. For such professionals being consciously aware, of their behaviour patterns or personality type and subsequently accepting the same, is the first meaningful step towards reducing dissonance and bringing synergy and happiness for themselves and others.

If such professionals reach senior or top management levels, they are most dangerous not only for the organization but also for teams they are managing. The next question that arises in our mind is – how can such people reach CEO or senior levels or do such people really reach those levels? The answer lies in keenly observing the past and present work-place landscape. Various prominently reported cases such as Enron or Lehman Brothers in the past and more recently, Renault-Nissan CEO or Cognizant bribery case in India and consequent fines and jails of their senior management professionals point to the fact that such people do reach top levels. Also, we must be conscious of the fact that these reported cases came to light whereas many may not have come to light.

Some unsuspecting professionals from among us, irrespective of levels, hierarchy or organization type, might have been victims of unscrupulous behaviours and designs of such professionals at one or other time in our careers. It is for these unsuspecting professionals from among us to be consciously aware of such senior professional's presence, behaviours and decisions and how we should use this conscious awareness to save ourselves from harm.

Consciously Preferred Behaviours

Understanding various personality types, cultures, synergies or dissonances, being consciously aware of the same is helpful only if we know, understand and are consciously self-aware of 'what matters to us' and whether our behaviour is organized accordingly. Conscious awareness enables us to understand that similar to personal life, corporate life too has preferred behaviour patterns which ensure inner peace of mind and personal development as well as outer synergy, harmony and professional growth through conscientious decision-making and mindful behaviours.

We, as consciously aware professionals, must be aware that a combination of Hercules, Aristotle, Professor and Passenger personality type behaviours are desirable or preferred behaviours in a work setting. However, we also needs to be aware that the combination of behaviours has to be in a right proportion depending on the role and level of hierarchy.

At a junior level, we are expected to be very hard-working, always willing to learn and be a good team-member. Such a role requires Hercules behaviours to be predominant with the other three behaviour patterns being displayed occasionally. When we reach middle management levels with some responsibility of managing team, we are expected to lead, plan and explain tasks to our team. This level's expectations can be ideally met by us if we are exhibiting Hercules behaviours but in lesser degree compared to junior levels. Our Aristotle and professor behaviours need to be higher compared to junior levels and at times, we should let the team execute the tasks by themselves, so we displaying passenger type behaviours in those times.

At a senior management level, the requirements of the role and expectations from professionals change. Apart from just delivering on targets, we need to provide leadership, direction and strategy, be a role model, collaborate with other senior leaders and manage conflicts among our team-members. At these levels, our Hercules behaviours need to reduce and pave way for Aristotle behaviours as dominant ones with Hercules and professor behaviours being next dominant ones. At times, when things are going as per plan, professionals at these levels need to behave similar to passenger personality to avoid over-pressurizing or micro-managing the teams at all times.

At CEO levels, we are expected to be the brain behind the entire business, utilize every team-member's skill-set optimally, let them execute the strategy once we have provided direction to the business and be a mentor and guide. The conscious awareness of role expectations enables us to understand that Aristotle behaviours must be the predominant ones in our behaviours at these levels.

A conscious transformation of ourselves at every stage of life is a very powerful and exciting thing to be undertaken. Breaking the word – transform, 'trans' means going beyond so effectively transforming ourselves implies going beyond our boundaries in changing ourselves. This transformation has to be a conscious transformation with knowledge, understanding and awareness of ourselves and the entire work-life and our conscious awareness that we are seeking happiness in our work-life.

Being consciously aware and making informed and conscious decision to transform ourselves at every stage of career not only results in higher professional productivity but also in synergies across hierarchies and cultures and consequent happiness for ourselves and others. A consciously aware professional will endeavour to move from being a predominantly Hercules to being a predominantly Aristotle personality as one moves from junior to senior levels, with professor (good communication) and passenger (considering a job as a job and not entire life) type behaviours in optimal proportions at all levels.

The behaviour traits of the rest of the four personalities not only bring dissonance for ourselves and make us unhappy but also vitiate the work-environment where we are working and create an unhappy work environment. Therefore those of us who display such behaviour traits in our personalities need to make conscious efforts to get rid of such behaviours and improve ourselves for being better human beings and professionals. This transformation can go a long way in our lives in making us more desirable as professionals, colleagues and managers. This state will bring a feeling of satisfaction and inner peace resulting in happiness for us as well those around us.

14. Happy Work-Life

Happiness is not something we postpone for the future, it is something we design for the present. A calm and modest work-life brings more happiness than the constant pursuit of professional success combined with incessant restlessness.

Through this journey of developing conscious awareness, we would have become consciously self-aware of priorities in life, priority of work-life motivational needs, and importance of ethical and moral values. Further, having understood own and other's personalities, it becomes easy to understand own behaviours and those of others and also how these personality differences lead to differences in ideas and behaviours. Similarly, as a consciously aware professional, we understand the reasons of differences with our manager and strive to develop understanding with the manager. Through conscious awareness, we can be aware of inner peace due to synergies and stress due to dissonance between self and others or between self and organizational culture.

For us, as professionals, accepting the truth that there is stress in corporate life due to dissonance, is the next step towards synergy, peace and harmony. Once we have accepted that there is dissonance, we need to dwell on the reasons of that dissonance in greater detail and be consciously aware of the same. These reasons can be either because of our inner self or because of outer behavioural interactions, conflicting value systems etc. However, conscious awareness enables us to understand that the dissonance is based on sound knowledge, understanding and conscious awareness of the reasons unlike previously held unfounded prejudices, fears, biases or expectations. Once we are consciously aware, we can focus on reducing stress to bring inner and outer peace, harmony and synergy.

Change what can be changed

A wise old proverb says, "Change what you can, accept what you can't and have the wisdom to know the difference."

In work-life, changing or adapting ourselves to the situation is within our control. Whereas changing our colleague's or manager's behaviour or existing organizational culture is not within our control. Knowing and being consciously aware of this difference is very important.

The next thing to be consciously aware of is how much of this dissonance or stress is because of us. It might be our expectations, behaviours, prejudices, value system etc. Managing our expectations based on logical and right priority of motivational needs helps us reduce the stress a lot and makes us happy. Similarly, behaving with high ethical and moral standards is the right behaviour but expecting the same from others may be walking into the territory of what can't be changed. Developing feelings of compassion, empathy, forgiveness for other's inappropriate behaviours, when those behaviours are within acceptable limits, instead of reacting to such behaviours helps us focus on important areas and reduce dissonance, stress and unhappiness.

Avoiding extreme behaviours always helps

If keenly observed, we can understand and realize that the stress in our work-life is not merely because of our expectations, prejudices or values but the extreme positions that we hold and the same being reflected in our behaviours that cause maximum stress and consequent unhappiness.

Perception of what constitutes an extreme behaviour can differ from one person to another. We always find two prominent cognitive bias in this perception. First, 'Self-serving bias' i.e. tendency to blame external forces when we display extreme behaviours and giving credit to ourselves when appropriate behaviours happen; second, Actor-observer bias i.e. tendency to attribute own extreme behaviours or reactions to external causes while attributing other's extreme behaviours to internal causes. These biases distort our perception of reasons of own and other's behaviours. This distorted perception is a major cause of unhappiness and therefore we must be objective while perceiving extreme behaviours.

Most of the times, it is not our beliefs, values and ideas or dislike of other's beliefs, values, ideas etc. that cause stress but when the same get reflected in our extreme behaviours, it becomes a reason of dissonance and consequent stress. For example, we may believe that a proposed business plan will result in losses and we may be right. Major dissonance and stress results when the same gets reflected in our compulsive behaviour of opposing it formally in all meetings and informally in discussions with colleagues. Once, we have given a differing opinion, not indulging in extreme behaviour of obsessively opposing it, is a consciously aware and mindful way of behaving.

Our extreme reactions to other professional's behaviour, events and situations lead to stressful and unhappy situations. For example, a colleague getting angry and expressing the same need not be reacted to or replied to in similar manner. Conscious awareness of that colleague's personality type, situation which led to that reaction and a mindful reaction of delaying the matter for some later day by being calm and composed may result in more consensus as well as avoidance of stressful and unhappy situation.

Avoiding extreme behaviours can be achieved by being consciously aware of other people's views, opinions, ideas and personalities and respecting them for who they are in spite of differences with them, instead of trying to make them agree to ourselves. Focusing on end-goals and not positions, listening, not reacting, managing own emotions consciously and having communication helps us avoid extreme behaviours and consequent unhappy situations.

Balancing-out expectations

All of us have expectations from work life, colleagues, manager or other stakeholders. These expectations are major cause of unhappiness for us because non-fulfilment of expectations leads to a feeling of either being cheated or used. Such feelings not only affect our inner peace but adversely affect our behaviours leading to major conflicting situations and dissonance.

For example, some of us who follows corporate etiquettes and are humble in behaviour expect the same from others. This might result in dissonance, stress and unhappiness because others may not be courteous or humble in their behaviours. Similarly, some of us who achieve targets expect a good appraisal. But our manager may hold biases and prejudiced perceptions against us or have strong personality differences with those of us who achieved targets and this may lead to a bad performance appraisal. This expectation of fairness leads to unhappiness.

We must balance-out our expectations. We may be courteous or may have contributed our hundred percent because that's our personality and integrity or values but the other stakeholder may not be having similar personality and value system. Can we control other's behaviours or how they do our performance appraisal? As consciously aware professionals, we must draw happiness from our behaviours and efforts because that is what we can control. External behaviours or events shouldn't be a factor in our happiness. Therefore as discussed in the first point, one must never focus on what is not in our control. The contentment and happiness has to come from our behaviour and values instead of making others emulate our behaviour or follow similar value system.

Having realistic expectations always helps. For example, it is very common for some of us that when we comes to know of higher salary of a colleague, a feeling of being less worthy or being slighted by manager or organization comes to mind. We need to be consciously aware of the circumstances and situations which led to such discrepancy such as better negotiating skills of our colleague or higher threshold when that colleague joined the organization or continuously over-achieving targets or great synergy between that professional and his/her manager. Having understood and become consciously aware of the circumstances and reasons, we must leverage this information constructively to convince the important stakeholders for a raise next time and also emphasizing that our knowing about this discrepancy isn't going to affect our commitment to organizational goals.

> "Do not spoil what you have by desiring what you have not; remember that what now you have was once among the things you only hoped for" – Epicurus.

Drawing boundaries of confirmation and agreement

Understanding people and culture logically and in a balanced manner and avoiding extreme behaviours by being consciously aware doesn't mean we need to confirm to or agree to everything that others say or believe. We must be consciously aware of basic tenants of our personality and value system as well as be consciously aware of areas where we won't compromise in any circumstances i.e. drawing our red lines.

For example, if our ethical principles don't allow us to compromise on financial honesty and integrity and legal compliances, then we must make these things clear through our words and actions. However, if we expect that all the colleagues and our manager must also be doing the same, then we may not be having a balanced and logical view of the situation. They have their own personalities and value systems and they will behave accordingly.

Having red-flags or drawing lines regarding acceptable behaviours or values helps us make crucial decisions which might be necessary to bring peace and happiness in our life. For example, we, as a Hercules or Aristotle professional, may face a dilemma when we need to decide between agreeing to manager's unreasonable demand of settling a new business deal through illegal dealings or moving to a non-descript job-role which will lead to job-loss i.e. jeopardizing our economic safety. Value-system related dilemmas are part and parcel of every corporate professional's life.

Having clarity about our red flags or boundaries of confirmation helps us in getting wake-up call in work-life to make conscientious and conscious decisions in such situations. These help us with clarity on what we will never do, irrespective of results. Ambiguity regarding decision-making results in confusion and stress whereas clarity of thoughts always brings inner peace and happiness.

Making and Accepting Decisions

Sometimes our conscious awareness makes us realize that our value system dissonance with the organizational culture or dissonance with manager or overall dissatisfaction and dissonance has reached a point wherein there are no chances of synergy, as much as we may try. If we can neither change this untenable dissonance nor accept the same, then it is time to say goodbye. In such circumstances, we must understand and be consciously aware that after all, this is just a job i.e. an economic activity to earn livelihood and this is just one part of life but not entire life. We need not persist with an untenable situation to a point where we are mentally and physically exhausted and professionally run-out of the steam.

Sometimes, it is better to move on than proving who was right. This might give us more peace and happiness. Choosing to leave a job, when it is the best option, is a path of empowerment and setting ourselves for better future. Once we have decided to quit or if we have already done it, we should 'celebrate the decision and be proud of it'. Because either we decided to give preference to our values and ethics or to our personal happiness or to our family and kids and each of these will add to our happiness.

Even if we were asked to quit because our hypocrite, free rider, mercenary or parasite personality type manager couldn't handle our passion, energy, knowledge, values or high ethical standards, we should be proud of ourselves instead of feeling regret as if we have lost something. We must be consciously aware that we didn't lose anything but it was the organization and manager who lost a great asset, whom they could have utilized for their own progress.

There may be situations when some of us might have decided to move on and started looking-out for avenues but still continued in the organization to ensure continuous economic security. In the meantime, manager decided to force our exit. In such situations, we need not feel any pain or belittlement but simply take it as advancement of an event which was certain to happen. In fact, this needs to be taken as an opportunity to focus completely on finding next assignment and feeling excited about a new beginning which will provide opportunities for new learning and meeting new people.

Sometimes, some of us become victims of corporate restructuring and have to leave job. In such cases, there is no need to feel slighted or feel that we weren't good enough. These are means of reducing costs in work-places and it had nothing to do with professional's skills, capabilities or knowledge. Someone, whom we didn't consider as good, might have stayed back owing to closeness to manager and that explains everything. Expecting that work-places, or world in general, has fairness and justice as core values is taking our expectations to unrealistic levels.

We need to be consciously aware of all these factors and never feel demotivated at all. Keeping our head high, believing in ourselves and starting again is what life is all about.

A lot of unhappiness in work-life results from not getting promoted and that even impacts our personal life adding to unhappiness of our near and dear ones. By making promotions as our happiness destinations, we are planning future unhappiness unconsciously because that is going to happen at some stage. It happens with everyone and we may find examples all around us. So, by accepting non-promotion as just part of everyone's professional life at some or other stage, sooner or later, we add immensely to our and our family's happiness.

Giving hundred percent is satisfying

"If a man is called a street-sweeper, he should sweep streets even as Michelangelo painted, or Beethoven composed music, or Shakespeare wrote poetry. He should sweep streets so well that all the hosts of heaven and earth will pause to say, here lived a great street-sweeper who did his job well." – Martin Luther King, Jr.

At a personal level, always doing our best is satisfying irrespective of the results because results aren't in our control but giving our best is. If we give our hundred percent, there are no regrets at a later stage such as, if I had put-in that extra effort or if I had done better, the results would have been better for me. Results are dependent not only on our efforts but on many other extraneous factors, which aren't in our control. Zig Ziglar appropriately summed-up this when he famously said – *"Winning is not everything, but the effort to win is."*

Committing ourselves to giving our hundred percent clears ambiguity and doubts from our mind i.e. should I do it or not. At the same time, it helps us control our reward expectations making ourselves more consciously aware of not being in control of rewards and also to the fact that our commitment itself is internally gratifying and satisfying.

This is another way of living in the moment i.e. the present instead of unnecessarily worrying about the future i.e. results. Whereas results might give satisfaction at some future point in time and keeps us worried till that time, hundred percent commitment provides everyday satisfaction and happiness in our work life. Happiness is not something that we should look for in future but it is a feeling for the present and living in the moment always makes us happy.

Celebrating our Uniqueness

Conscious awareness enables us to be aware of the fact that every one of us is unique with our priorities of life, priority of motivational needs, skills, behaviours and strengths and weaknesses. We must endeavour to work positively on our weaknesses and behavioural extremes. However, this endeavour shouldn't hamper celebration of our uniqueness, our positivity and what we have.

As a consciously aware professional, we must celebrate our uniqueness and positivity, enjoys small things in life, neither get too excited about work-life success nor get too disappointed with not so successful moments, prioritize our motivational needs and resulting behaviours as per our consciously aware priorities of life. For us, life is more about being happy through living it fully everyday with enthusiasm, honesty, dedication, joyfulness and in a consciously aware way.

*

"No problem can be solved from the same level of consciousness that created it." – Albert Einstein

In order to bring happiness in our work-life, we need to overcome stress and unhappiness caused by inner dissonance, daily behavioural confusions, stress causing human dynamics and decision-making dilemmas in work-place. For doing the same, we need to move to the next level of consciousness which is conscious awareness of our work-life.

We, as consciously aware professionals, continually seek harmonious relationships with ourself and those around i.e. family, loved ones, friends, colleagues etc. We must do so through better knowledge, understanding and conscious awareness of our inner and outer self and surrounding environment, be it family, social or work-life.

Through conscious self-awareness, we gain clarity regarding our priority of needs as well as our behaviours and actions, which are always in synergy with our true needs. We must endeavour to avoid dissonance and consequent unhappiness by displaying balanced behaviours, developing conscious understanding and acceptance of others and conscientious decision-making.

Instead of looking persistently for change, we must decide for change with full conscious awareness of the reasons thereof and when the change happens, we must accept it and be willing to transform ourselves.

The journey of happiness through conscious awareness is a continuous journey and if we, as professionals, walk on this path persistently, it will lead to inner and outer harmony and happiness and also our personal, professional and spiritual growth.

"A man is but the product of his thoughts; what he thinks, he becomes." – Mahatma Gandhi

*

Bibliography

1. Easwaran, Eknath (2007). The Bhagavad Gita: Classics of Indian Spirituality. Nilgiri Press
2. Uchida, Y., Kitayama, S. (2009). Happiness and unhappiness in east and west: themes and variations. Emotion, 9(4), 441-456
3. Csikszentmihalyi, M. (2002). Flow: The classic work on how to achieve happiness. Random House
4. Wierzbicko, A. (2004). 'Happiness' in cross-linguistic & cross-cultural perspective. Daedalus, 133(2), 34-43
5. Golman, D. (2009). Emotional Intelligence: Why it can matter more than IQ. India: Bloomsbury Publication
6. Fowler, Jeaneane D. (2012). The Bhagawad Gita: A Text and Commentary for Students, Sussex Academic Press
7. Sims, R.R. and Brinkmann, J. (2003). Enron Ethics (or: Culture matters more than codes). Journal of Business Ethics, 45(3), 243-256
8. Robbins, S.P. and Judge, T.A. (2009). Organizational Behavior (13th ed.). Upper Saddle River, NJ: Pearson Education Inc.
9. Truxillo, D.M., Bauer, T.N. and Erdogan, B. (2016). Psychology and work: Perspectives on Industrial and Organizational Psychology. New York: Routledge
10. Kluckohn, Clyde. (1959). Mirror for Man: The Relation of Anthropology to Everyday Life. McGraw Hill.
11. Peter Randall (2013). The Psychology of Feeling Sorry: The Weight of the Soul. pp. 206-208.
12. Duval, Shelley and Wicklund, Robert A (1972). A Theory of Objective Self-awareness, Academic Press
13. Harter, Susan (1999). The Construction of the Self, Guilford Press

14. https://thepolicytimes.com/whos-workplace-rules-for-happy-life/
15. https://www.mediate.com/articles/belak4.cfm#
16. www.thebuddhagarden.com
17. www.vocabulary.com
18. www.businessdictionary.com
19. www.collinsdictionary.com
20. www.oxforddictionaries.com
21. www.merriam-webster.com/dictionary
22. Taleb, Nassim Nicholas (2007). The Black Swan: the impact of the highly improbable. London: Penguin
23. Maslow, A.H. (1943). A Theory of Human Motivation. Psychological Review, 50(4), 370-96
24. Maslow, A.H. (1954). Motivation and Personality. New York: Harper and Row
25. Maslow, A.H. (1987). Motivation and Personality (3rd ed.). Delhi, India: Pearson Education
26. Krings, Franciska & Bollmann, Gregoire. (2011). Managing counterproductive work behaviors.

About the authors

Raj Bhambu is a business leader with 23 years of varied corporate experience in MNCs, banking and as an Army Officer with Indian Army. He did his MBA in Advanced Strategy from Lancaster University Management School, UK.

Anshu Choudhary is an author, painter and experienced human dynamics professional with extensive humanities education through her Masters in Psychology, MBA in HRD and PG Diploma in Human Rights and Diploma in Urdu Language.

www.ingramcontent.com/pod-product-compliance
Lightning Source LLC
Chambersburg PA
CBHW032013170526
45157CB00002B/683